"The market can stay irrational much longer than you can stay solvent"
(John Maynard Keynes)

"I'd be a bum on the street with a tin cup if the markets were always
efficient" (Warren Buffett)

"Ничего не хоти, умрешь веселым" (Елизавета Быликина)

©2014 by Vasily Nekrasov
Hohewartstr. 7
71144 Steinenbronn
Germany

ISBN 978-3-00-046520-8
http://www.yetanotherquant.com

Contents

Preface

There are thousands of books on trading[1]. For instance, the query "trading" yielded (on 04.02.2014) 62986 results on amazon.com. However, the content is extremely repetitive from book to book. First of all most of them sell hope, not knowledge. It is actually obvious: a professional writer (professional in the sense that he writes for a living) wants his books to be sold. It is much easier to sell hope than knowledge (which is often bitter) to a mass reader. Such books usually tell you that there are several markets (equities, commodities, bonds, FX) and either one of these markets is claimed to suit a private trader particularly well or it is recommended to concentrate on profit opportunities, not on asset classes. Then comes a common warning that "most time the markets are unpredictable", or alternatively an encouragement that the stock prices grow in the long term. Then some very basic information on brokers and trading orders, probably something on fundamental analysis and market psychology. Most of these books are about technical analysis such as chart patterns, since the quantitative indicators like moving averages require some mathematics, which the most of mass readers do not possess.

As to concrete trading strategy recommendations, they are distinctly clustered (and sorted in order of the cluster size) as follows: nothing concrete, trend following, swing trading, buy and hold, pair/spread trading and "exotics" like seasonal trading and chasing penny stocks. With very few exceptions no book contains a detailed strategy description. But even if the latter is there, there is still no word about the backtesting. Money management is either completely disregarded or its importance is noted but without detailed arguments. Concrete recommendations are rare, the rules of thumb are to not risk more than x% of the capital per trade (x% is often 1% or 2%, sometimes up to 5%). Another common advice is to take the volatility into account but all they recommend is usually just to take smaller positions in volatile stocks.

On the other hand there are a lot of books on "modern" quantitative finance. While the most of them are mathematically flawless, their content is both unreadable for a mere mortal and has little to do with

---

[1] In this book the words "investment" and "trading" are used interchangeably.

reality. And of course they are very costly; $100+ is not an uncommon price.

In this sense this book is brand new. First of all, it does not sell hope and is not intended for "dummies". Rather it is for retail investors who already have some experience. It is also very useful for students who study [quantitative] finance. In order to read this book, you need a *working* knowledge of college mathematics[2]. On the other hand, this book is practically oriented and completely void of mathematical arrogance. Moreover, the content of the chapters 2 and 3 is very elementary but at the same time thoroughly explained. Even if you cope only with these chapters, the book is worth its price since you get a clear perception of what you can (and what you cannot) achieve in the market in the long term.

Modern investment is unthinkable without modern IT, so some programming skills are very helpful (though not necessary if you are ready to learn in parallel).

This book does not present any out of box super winning strategy (though I do disclose my personal investment approach). Such strategies - even if they do work - expire quickly. However, this book does provide you with a toolset to create (and what is more important, to test and evaluate) trading strategies.

I also take into account that (like me) the most of my readers have a fulltime job and a family. This implies that a *practical* investment activity should not be too time-consuming. For those, who are too busy and have very little time but still wish to invest this book provides some hints how to avoid common errors and pitfalls.

Since I live in Germany, I mostly watch the German market. Thus most of the examples are about German stocks. Though the German market does have its peculiarities (strong dependence on export, conservatism of German investors), these examples are straightforwardly applicable for any developed market.

---

[2]I mean US college level, which is approximately equal to the German Abitur or Russian high-school with emphasis on math.

Finally, it is worth explaining what motivated me to write this book. Well, first of all "when a man has anything to tell in this world, the difficulty is not to make him tell it, but to prevent him from telling it"[3]. Like every person I also want my efforts to be rewarded. However, I expect the main profit not from the book sales but rather from the increase in my goodwill: being an author of a *good* book usually helps in career. Keeping the book price under €15 I try to make it affordable for everyone and in particular for students. I hope this book will be interesting and useful to the readers and help to navigate in turbulent financial markets.

Writing a book is always a big undertaking, which requires a lot of time and concentration. This book would never be written without my wife Olesja who inspired and supported me all the time. Karla Penter did her best to translate my "Russian English" to the British English (all remained typos and grammar mistakes are completely my fault, not hers). I am very indebted to Dr. Thomas Rupp for his valuable remarks.

In order to improve the book I actively used ~~crowd~~folksourcing. I am grateful to everybody who has contributed, in particular to Matthias Siemering, Jörg Hiermayr, Dimitri Semenchenko, Dmitriy Bogdanis, Dr. Frank Wittemann, Dr. Peter Schwendner, Dr. Roland Stamm, Dr. Aleksey Min, Natalia Shenkman, Stanislav Narivonchik, Alex Ocnariu, Alexander Mora Araya, Daniel Lamparter, Daniel Schroeter, Elena Tichij, Florin Leist, Franziska Zerweck, Gloria Straub, Laila Unkauf, Oksana Mook, Roman Wenger, Sekou Cissé, Christiane Kandeler, Celine de Sousa and Vincenzo de Matteo.

---

[3] Caesar and Cleopatra by George Bernard Shaw
(http://www.gutenberg.org/files/3329/3329-h/3329-h.htm#link2H_4_0003).

Chapter 1: A brief review of the probability theory

As I warned you, you need a working knowledge of college mathematics in order to read this book. For the sake of completeness, we briefly review the main ideas of the probability theory. We start with a quiz, which although elementary is not trivial. Moreover, it addresses both the typical problems you will encounter as an investor and some fine ideas of probability theory that often remain beyond the scope of the first course on probability. If the quiz is no problem for you then neither will be the rest of the book. But if you cannot comprehend it even after reading the solutions then... well, you might still succeed as investor. I know a couple of people that have trouble with this quiz but are still successful on the market (or at least they say that they are). However, I believe the investment should be a healthy blend of science and life experience rather than a curios mixture of subconsciousness and voodoo craft.

Q1: Initial prices of stocks A and B were, respectively, $10 and $100. Later the prices grew, respectively, to $20 and $150. Which stock performed better?

Q2: A portfolio consists of three stocks; their weights in portfolio are equal. After a year the first stock yielded 15%, the second -20% and the third one 10%. What is portfolio's total return?

Q3: A trader invested his capital in an ETF[4] on RTS[5]. The return for the first year was 10%, for the second year 15% but for the third year -20%. After the third year a trader sold his portfolio. How much has he earned?

Q4: A similar situation as by Q3 but now the returns were -20%, 15% and 10%. Does the order of returns really matter?

---

[4] Exchange Traded Fund
[5] Russian stock index

Q5: A stock dropped by $x\%$ then grew by $y\%$ and returned to its initial price. Write a formula to express y via x.

Q6: A trader bought a stock, held it for three months and then sold, yielding 5%. What is his annualized growth rate?

Q7: If we want to double our wealth in five years, which annualized growth rate do we need?

Q8: One thousand people took a new medicine. One of them had an allergic reaction. What is the probability of the allergic response?

Q9: A deck consists of 36 cards[6]. What are the probabilities a) to get a queen, b) to get spades, c) to get the queen of spades?

Q10: One has tossed a coin ten times and got ten heads. What is the probability to get a head by the eleventh toss?

Q11: The first bank account pays 6% annually, the second pays 3% semi-annually, the third pays 1.5% quarterly and the fourth pays 0.5% monthly. Which bank account is better (assuming they all can be considered risk-free)?

---

[6] Such "abridged" decks are most common in Russia. There are 9 values from six to ace and 4 suits.

A1: The return on the first stock is (20-10)/10 = 1 = 100%, whereas the return on the second stock is (150-100)/100 = 0.5 = 50%. Thus the first stock has performed better. The absolute price changes (in this case, respectively, $10 and $50) do not matter: if an investor has, e.g. $100, he can buy either ten stocks A or one stock B. In the first case his gain will be 10*$10 = $100 and in the second case just 1*$50=$50.

A2: Assume a trader initially had x dollars. The stock weights in portfolio are equal, i.e. he has invested $x/3$ dollars in each stock. His terminal wealth is then (1+0.15)x/3 + (1-0.2)x/3 + (1+0.1)x/3 = (3 + 0.05)x/3 = x + 0.0167x. Since his initial capital was x, the total return is equal to (x + 0.0167x - x) / x = 0.0167. Of course we could just have calculated the [simple] average of returns: (0.15 - 0.2 + 0.1) / 3 = 0.0167 = 1.67%. In general, the weights of stocks in a portfolio are not the same. In this case the portfolio return is equal to $\sum_{i=1}^{n} w_i r_i / \sum_{i=1}^{n} w_i$, where w_i and r_i are the weight and the return of the i-th stock.

A3: Assume a trader initially had x dollars. After the first year the return was 10%, so the total wealth after the first year is x + 0.1x =x(1+0.1)= 1.1x . The return for the second year was 15% and a trader had 1.1x dollars at the beginning of the second year. That is, his wealth at the end of the second year is 1.1x(1+0.15) = 1.265x . Analogously, the wealth at the end of the third year is 1.265x(1-0.2) = 1.012x . So the total return is 1.2%. And the *annualized* return (s. A6) is just 0.4%. The lesson from Q2 and Q3: never confuse an arithmetic mean and a compound annual growth rate (CAGR).

A4: As you likely noticed, the formula to calculate the total return for the case of Q3 is (1+0.1)(1+0.15)(1-0.2) - 1 . Since the product is commutative, the order of annual returns does not matter. However, it likely matters from a psychological point of view: especially for a newbie the scenario -20%, 15%, 10% is much less comfortable than 10%, 15%, -20%. As a matter of fact, most of trading software displays only the acquisition price and the current price. So in the first case a trader will always see a profit. Though the profit decreases from 26.5% to 1.2%, comparing the acquisition price with the current price we are still in the black. But in the second case we first need to endure the loss of 20%. Note that the experienced traders usually consider the *maximum drawdown*, which does not depend on the order of returns and is equal to -20% in both cases. Further we will use the maximum drawdown as the main measure of risk.

A5: It holds: 1 = (1-x)(1+y) thus $y = \dfrac{1}{1-x} - 1$

Let us calculate some concrete values, which you should learn by heart:

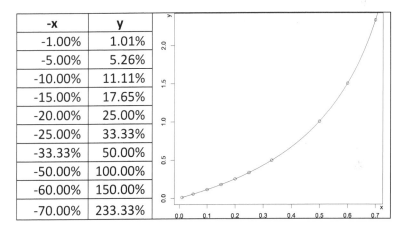

-x	y
-1.00%	1.01%
-5.00%	5.26%
-10.00%	11.11%
-15.00%	17.65%
-20.00%	25.00%
-25.00%	33.33%
-33.33%	50.00%
-50.00%	100.00%
-60.00%	150.00%
-70.00%	233.33%

A6: The question is not as elementary as it may seem to be. First of all, the answer depends on the so-called day count convention. The simplest one is 30/360, i.e. for simplicity's sake we assume 30 days in every month and 360 days in every year. Thus [any] three months make exactly a quarter of year and it holds: $(1+r)^{0.25} = 1.05$ Taking logs we obtain $0.25\ln(1+r) = \ln(1.05) = 0.04879$ Exponentiate and get $1+r = \exp(0.19516) = 1.21550$ Finally $r = 0.21550$ We check the solution: $(1+0.21550)^{0.25} = 1.04999865 \approx 1.05$

The general formula 1-A6-1 is not the only feasible one (s. A11). However, it is most common in [practical] finance.

$$(1 + r)^t = 1 + R$$

$$r = \exp\left(\frac{\ln(1 + R)}{t}\right) - 1$$

Formula 1-A6-1 CAGR or the annualization of the interest rate R accrued during the time t.

Note that the 5% that was yielded after the three months are called [quarterly] *simple return*. The average (or the arithmetic mean) of the simple returns over several periods is called *arithmetic return*. The arithmetic return is an important number for a series of bets (or trades) *without* reinvestment of winnings. It is also used to find the optimal portfolios (s. the chapter on Kelly criterion). But in order to characterize a series of trades with reinvestments we need CAGR or, alternatively, a *geometric mean* return over several periods (CAGR is more convenient since it also allows to compare two strategies with different investment periods).

A7: It holds $(1 + r)^5 = 2$ thus according to the formula 1-A6-1 $r = 0.14870$ which is pretty ambitious. For comparison: the DAX (German counterpart of Dow Jones Industrial Average) has a long-term CAGR about 8%. On the other hand Warren Buffet achieves 20% CAGR.

A8: This question is not trivial. A correct but an incomplete answer is as follows: one in a thousand is 0.1% thus the probability of the allergic response is also 0.1%. According to Thilo Sarrazin only 46%

of Germans and 25% of Americans can provide this answer[7]. The problem is, however, that 0.1% is just an empirical estimation of the [genuine] probability but not the genuine probability itself. The more the number of trials (in this case the number of persons that took the medicine) the better is the convergence of the estimate to the genuine probability. The underlying theory is far from being easy. Fortunately there is an accessible alternative: the Monte Carlo simulation, which will be one of the most important tools for us.

A9: Among 36 cards there are 4 queens. For a well-shuffled deck each card can be drawn with equal probability, which is 1/36. In four cases there can be a queen, so the total probability is 4/36 = 1/9 = 11.11%. Analogously there are 9 spades thus the probability to get a spade is 1/4 = 25%. Finally, there is only one queen of spades, so the probability to get it is 1/36 = 2.78%. Note that the suit of a card is obviously independent from its value. On the other hand the probability to draw the queen of spades is numerically equal to the product of probabilities to draw a queen and to draw spades. In general, if the events A and B are independent then the probability that both A and B will occur is equal to the product of their probabilities. Moreover, the converse is also true, i.e. if the formula 1-A9-1 holds then the events A and B are independent.

$$\mathbb{P}(AB) = \mathbb{P}(A)\mathbb{P}(B)$$

Formula 1-A9-1 Probability law for independent events

A10: This case is a perfect demonstration of the "contradictions" between the empirical and the genuine probability or, as some people say, between mathematics and physics. A "physicist" will conclude that the coin is heavily biased, so the probability to get a

---

[7] T. Sarrazin, "Deutschland schafft sich ab". 6th ed(2010), p. 196
Thilo Sarrazin (born in 1945) was a very successful senator for finance in Berlin and a member of the Executive Board of the German Central Bank (Bundesbank).

head by the next toss shall be close to 1. However, a "mathematician" will assume a fair coin and thus state that the probability to get a head by the 11th toss is still 0.5, since the toss outcomes are independent from each other[8]. Note that *if* the coin is fair, the probability to get 10 heads by 10 tosses is, according to the formula 1-A9-1 equal to $(0.5)^{10} = 0.0009765625 \approx 0.1\%$. It is experience and not mathematics that lets us decide whether to consider an event virtually impossible or pretty rare but still possible. In case of a *fair* coin I would rather say, it is virtually impossible to get 10 heads by 10 tosses. But an allergic reaction of one patient among one thousand does not imply (at least to me) that the allergy is virtually impossible, though the probability of this event is 0.1% as well... Continuing on with this idea, there is one more example, which I learnt from the wonderful textbook on probability theory by Elena Wenzel[9]: if you are an artillerist, you likely can accept that one of a thousand shells will not explode by hitting a target. But if you are a paratrooper, the probability of 0.1% to have your parachute undeployed will likely be too high for you.

A11: The first bank account pays 6% return to the end of the year. The second pays off $(1 + 0.03)^2 = 1.0609$ (first payment takes place after six months and the second to the end of the year). Analogously for the third account we have $(1 + 0.015)^4 = 1.06136$ and $(1 + 0.005)^{12} = 1.06168$ for the fourth. So there is a difference, although not really a big one. What if we continue this process to its limit (and does this limit exist at all)?! Yes, it does! This is known as *continuously compounded interest* and it is very popular in the theory of mathematical finance.

$$\lim_{n \to \infty} \left(1 + \frac{r}{n}\right)^{\frac{t}{n}} = \exp(rt)$$

Formula 1-A11-1 Continuously compounded interest

---

[8] In other words they are serially independent.
[9] Elena Sergeevna Wentzel (1907-2002) was a prominent Soviet mathematician and writer (she wrote under pseudonym I. Grekova that literally means "Mrs. Y").

We can also obtain the formula 1-A11-1 the other way around. Assume that the wealth in a bank account grows proportionally to its current value W_t with coefficient r, i.e. the following differential equation holds: $dW_t = rW_t dt$. The solution is $W_t = W_0 \exp(rt)$ where W_0 is the initial wealth.

Very close is the idea of the *logarithmic returns*, i.e. if the initial wealth was W_0 , the terminal wealth is equal to W_1 and the investment period was t years then the logarithmic return is

$$r = \frac{1}{t} \ln \left(\frac{W_1}{W_0} \right) = \frac{\ln(W_1) - \ln(W_0)}{t}$$

Formula 1-A11-2 Logarithmic returns

Indeed, if the interest is compounded continuously then $W_1 = W_0 \exp(rt)$ thus 1-A11-A2 holds. Logarithmic returns are convenient for continuous time models[10]. Since the stock trading is essentially discrete, we will mostly use compound returns according to 1-A6-1.

Now we turn to the probability theory. As you may know, it originates from gambling. The easiest case is a symmetric coin: the probabilities of head (H) and tail (T) are both equal to 0.5. However, the question "what is the probability to get *at least* one head if we toss a symmetric coin twice" is not completely trivial. Still we can enumerate all possible outcomes. They are HH, HT, TH and TT. The first three outcomes suit our criterion. Since the coin is symmetric, they all have the same probability, which is equal to 0.25; recall that the probabilities of all possible (and mutually exclusive) outcomes

---

[10] In particular due to the fact that a compound return on a long and non-leveraged position can take values in [-1, ∞], whereas a logarithmic return can lie in [−∞, ∞] and thus can be straightforwardly modeled by continuous probability distribution like the normal distribution.

must sum to one. Thus the probability of the event to get at least one head by two tosses is 0.75 or 75%.

So far so good but what if we want to calculate, say, the probability to get at least 60 heads by 100 tosses?! The enumeration of the outcomes does not seem to be feasible anymore. We still could have solved this problem analytically but we actually need not. Instead we can engage R, an opensource and royalty-free statistical software.

```
#exact value
print("Exact Solution")
1 - pbinom(59, 100, 0.5)

#approximate value by Monte Carlo simulation
tosses = rbinom(100000, 100, 0.5)
nSuccessfulOutcomes = 0
for(i in 1:100000)
{
  if(tosses[i] >=60 )
    nSuccessfulOutcomes = nSuccessfulOutcomes + 1
}
print("Approximate Solution")
nSuccessfulOutcomes / 100000
```
R-code 1.1 Probability of at least 60 heads by 100 tosses

If you never heard about R before, don't worry. So far just go to http://www.r-project.org, download and install R (the installation on Windows is straightforward) and enter the R-code 1.1 to the command line. Further we will learn the basics of R iteratively step by step. Let us discuss the R-code 1.1 in detail. The command pbinom(59, 100, 0.5) in the 3rd line gives the exact value of the probability that there will be no more than 59 heads by 100 tosses of a symmetric coin (0.5 stands for the probability of head). Respectively, the probability that there will be 60 or more heads is 1 - pbinom(59, 100, 0.5) .

Here we made use of our knowledge of the probability distribution. But this will not always be the case. For example, we may draw the stock returns from a (sophisticated) distribution and have no idea of the distribution of terminal wealth (though the distribution of returns is known). But it is absolutely no problem as long as we have R at hand[11]. All we need to do is just to run a Monte Carlo simulation, which is, in our case, nothing else but a computer simulation of the coin tosses. The command `tosses = rbinom(100000, 100, 0.5)` tells R to simulate 100 tosses of a symmetric coin, calculate the sum of heads, repeat the process 100000 times and put the values to the array "tosses". Command `nSuccessfulOutcomes = 0` initiates the counter of outcomes with 60 heads or more. Then we run through all outcomes with a *for*-loop and check whether we got the desired number of heads. If yes, we increment *nSuccessfulOutcomes* by one. In the last code line `nSuccessfulOutcomes / 100000` we divide the number of successful outcomes by the total number of trials. The more it is, the better the final result converges to the genuine probability of the event to get 60 heads or more.

In my case the genuine probability was 0.02844397 (and will obviously be the same in your case). As to the approximate probability, I yielded 0.02896 which is pretty close to the genuine value. However, in your case it will be slightly different, though most likely also close to the true value.

If you are completely new to programming, do the following:
1. Read more about arrays (in principle, an array is just a sequence of values).
2. Read about loops (loops are used to repeat the same or the similar actions many times). Besides *for*-loop, learn also *while*-loop.
3. Learn the conditional operator *if* and its extension *if ... else* as well as logical operators *and*, *or*, *not* (in R they are, respectively, written as &&, ||, !) .
4. Note the difference of the assignment operator = and its synonym <- vs. "equal to" operator == .

Exercise 1.1 (programming)

---

[11] The only problem we may encounter is the computational intensity.

By means of this simple Monte Carlo simulation we addressed two important topics: the (discrete) stochastic processes and (the convergence to) the expectation of a random variable. Let us so far postpone the former and discuss the latter. If we assign 1 to head and 0 to tail, the expected value of a single coin toss is 0.5. Recall the definition of the expectation:

$$\mathbb{E}[X] := \sum_{i=1}^{n} p_i X_i$$

Definition 1.1 Expectation of a discrete random variable

where X_i is the value of a random variable in case of outcome i and p_i is the probability of this outcome. In our example let[12] $X_1 := \{X = T\} = 0$, $X_2 := \{X = H\} = 1$
Since the coin is symmetric, $p_1 = p_2 = 0.5$ and $\mathbb{E}[X] = p_1 X_1 + p_2 X_2 = 0.5 \cdot 0 + 0.5 \cdot 1 = 0.5$
Note that sometimes we can calculate the expectation just by intuition[13]. Indeed, if we toss a symmetric coin 100 times, we should get approximately the same number of heads and tails. Since we assigned 1 to head and 0 to tail, the expectation is 50.

Now let us note a very important idea, which you (or your instructor) may have missed out in your first course on probability.

> In case of a <u>single</u> toss (or just <u>a few</u> tosses) the expectation is not really meaningful!

---

[12] ":=" means "equal by definition". The expression $X_1 := \{X = T\}$ is read as follows: by definition let the first outcome take place when we got a tail by a coin toss.

[13] But be careful, in mathematics the intuition can easily let you down! That's why always verify it by a Monte Carlo simulation!

Indeed, the expectation is just the average value, but does averaging really make sense in case of just one coin toss? The situation radically changes if we toss a coin many times (the more, the better). By hundred tosses the probability to get *exactly* the expected value, i.e. 50, is about 8% which does not seem to be very large. However, the probability that the outcome deviates from the expected value by no more than ±10 is more than 95%! You can check it with R command pbinom(60, 100, 0.5) - pbinom(39,100,0.5). It means that in a sense *the random outcome becomes less and less random as we increase the number of trials*. In other words the mean value of the experiment converges to its expectation.

Here we smoothly step to the next important concept: the variance and the standard deviation (that are direct relatives of the assets volatility). Let us slightly modify our example: instead of a coin toss consider a stock A, which can either fall 5% down or grow 10% up. Further let stock B go either 30% up or 25% down. Note that in practice we can often estimate these numbers relatively precisely and even *define* them, e.g. if we set our take profit and stop loss orders accordingly[14]. Let the probabilities[15] of both events be 0.5. According to the definition 1.1 both stocks have the same expected return. Indeed: $0.5 \cdot 0.1 + 0.5 \cdot (-0.05) = 0.025 = 2.5\%$ and $0.5 \cdot 0.3 + 0.5 \cdot (-0.25) = 0.025 = 2.5\%$.

However, you (should) intuitively feel that the stock B is much more risky. Indeed, for both stocks we expect the same return but we know that by the stock A we will not lose more than 5% of our investment even in the worst case. Or in other words, the worst possible deviation from the expected return is equal to -7.5%. But for the stock B it is -27.5%!

---

[14] Of course there is always a chance that the traded asset will reach neither stop loss nor take profit. However, experienced traders rarely encounter this case, later we will discuss why.

[15] As to the probabilities, they are really hard to estimate. However, it is not an insuperable hindrance. Later we will consider how to deal with it.

At this point we are getting somewhat messy since we mix the variance and the (maximum) drawdown risk. They are not the same. However, as long as the returns never deviate too far from their expectations[16], the drawdown risk and the variance are very closely related! You will see this in the next chapter.

Stop reading for a while and have a cup of tea. Imagine that you have lost 5% of your savings. How do you feel? Now imagine that the loss is 25%. Have you planned to buy a house or a new car? Or maybe an expensive vacation? Which loss would be acceptable for you so that you still could afford all your plans?
Exercise 1.2 (psychology)

Now let us formally define the variance and the standard deviation.

$$\mathbb{VAR}[X] := \mathbb{E}[(X - \mathbb{E}[X])^2]$$

Definition 1.2 Variance of a random variable

$$\text{StdDev}[X] := \sqrt{\mathbb{VAR}[X]}$$

Definition 1.3 Standard deviation of a random variable

Essentially, *the standard deviation measures the dispersion of the outcomes from their expected value.* You may wonder why we at first consider $\mathbb{E}[(X - \mathbb{E}[X])^2]$ and then take the square root instead of simply considering $\mathbb{E}[(X - \mathbb{E}[X])]$. As a matter of fact, $\mathbb{E}[(X - \mathbb{E}[X])] = 0$ (as a good exercise, prove this statement! Just apply the definition 1.1. As a useful corollary you will get that

---

[16] Or, in mathematical terms, as long as the return distribution has no fat tails.

$\mathbb{E}[\mathbb{E}[X]] = \mathbb{E}[X]$ and, in general, the expectation of a constant is this constant itself). Additionally, the advantages of the definitions 1.2 and 1.3 become evident as soon as one encounters the *linear regression*.

Let us calculate the variance of returns on stocks A and B. For convenience, we summarize the possible outcomes and their probabilities. In other words, we specify the probability distributions for the random returns of the both stocks.

Probability	Return on stock A	Return on stock B
0.5	-0.05	-0.25
0.5	0.1	0.3

We have already calculated that $\mathbb{E}[A] = \mathbb{E}[B] = 0.025$ According to the definitions 1.2 and 1.3, we calculate
$\mathbb{VAR}[A] = 0.5 \cdot (0.1 - 0.025)^2 + 0.5 \cdot (-0.05 - 0.025)^2 = 0.005625$
$\mathbb{VAR}[B] = 0.5 \cdot (0.3 - 0.025)^2 + 0.5 \cdot (-0.25 - 0.025)^2 = 0.075625$
Hence $\mathrm{StdDev}[A] = 0.075$ and $\mathrm{StdDev}[B] = 0.275$

Chapter 2: Money Management according to Kelly criterion: the first encounter

Every highly qualified telecommunication engineer knows the (basics of) information theory. This theory does not tell him how to design the devices with the maximum bandpass but it does tell him which bandpass he can theoretically achieve. Since our engineer is highly qualified, he knows that practically achievable bandpass will be somewhat below the theoretical one.

We - the financiers - have our own analogue of the information theory that tells us, which maximum expected growth rate, i.e. which CAGR, we can achieve in the long term. This "fortune's formula" is known as Kelly criterion. Surprisingly, it was Claude Shannon (the father of the information theory), who significantly contributed to its discovery. Even more surprising is that very few financial professionals are (really) aware about Kelly criterion. At the same time every gambler knows it.

A short historical review of Kelly criterion is quite appropriate here[17]. The original paper "A New Interpretation of Information Rate"[18] was written by J. L. Kelly, JR. in 1956. In essence, it considers a favorable game[19] and the optimal fraction of gambling capital, which one should bet by each stake. But from the traders' and bettors' point of view the published version is pretty vague. Though one can grasp the main idea, the paper is rather about communication channels than about optimal stakes. Allegedly, there was an earlier version, written both by Kelly and Shannon. In this version the author(s) freely talked about bookies and insiders. But both authors worked for AT&T, whose management "was never

---

[17] For the most part I follow James Case's paper "The Kelly Criterion: Fallacy or Kuhnian Paradigm Shift Waiting to Happen?" (SIAM News, Volume 39, Number 3, April 2006, available at http://www.siam.org/pdf/news/930.pdf)

[18] Available at https://www.princeton.edu/~wbialek/rome/refs/kelly_56.pdf

[19] Favorable game is a game with a positive expectation. The simplest case is tossing of a non-symmetric coin. Oppositely, in case of a symmetric coin the expectation is zero, so one speaks about *fair* game.

keen to advertise the fact that bookies long represented an embarrassingly large fraction of the firm's customer base". As a result, the authors prepared a "more politically correct" version, signed by Kelly alone.

A couple of years later Edward Thorp[20], a professor of mathematics at MIT found out how to get an edge in blackjack. Shannon was a good friend of Thorp and drew his attention to Kelly's paper. Kelly's approach allowed Thorp to maximize *in long term* the advantage of his edge in blackjack. Thorp applied his strategy in Las Vegas casinos and made good money. Successful gamblers are quickly recognized and expelled from casinos, so Thorp had to disguise himself in a combination of wraparound glasses and a beard in order to avoid expulsion.

Yet a casino affair was just a warm-up for Thorp. His real deal was the statistical arbitrage, i.e. the exploration of the market imperfections that though not necessarily guarantees a riskless profit but provides a sure edge "on average". In an efficient market there are no such imperfections but Thorp never believed the markets were efficient. ‹‹In the late 1970s affordable, powerful computers and high quality databases were becoming more affordable, making a revolution in Finance possible... The idea was to rank stocks by their percentage change in price, corrected for splits and dividends, over a recent past period such as the last two weeks. We found that the stocks that were most up tended to fall relative to the market over the next few weeks and the stocks which were the most down tended to rise relative to the market. Using this forecast our computer simulations showed approximately a 20 percent annualized return from buying the "best" decile of stocks, and selling short the "worst" decile[21]››. Prof. Thorp is a seminal writer; however, he never disclosed *in detail* how he applied Kelly criterion to his portfolio of *many* assets. We will

---

[20] http://en.wikipedia.org/wiki/Edward_O._Thorp

[21] Ed Thorp, A Mathematician on Wall Street. Statistical Arbitrage - Part II. http://www.wilmott.com/pdfs/080630_thorp.pdf

discuss this issue later but so far consider the Kelly criterion in its simplest univariate form.

Assume a gambler tosses a biased coin so that the probability p to get a tail is known and larger than 0.5. (In our terms, it is a favorable game and a gambler has an edge). After each bet a gambler loses or doubles the money at stake. Obviously, he wants to exploit his edge completely and at first glance the idea to maximize his *expected terminal wealth* (recall definition 1.1) does not look implausible. Let W_0 be his initial capital and let u be the fraction that the gambler bets at each stake. Respectively, he lays aside *(1-u)*. Then the expected capital after the first bet is

$$W_0[2pu + (1 - p) \cdot 0 + (1 - u)] = W_0[2pu + 1 - u]$$

Respectively, the expected capital after the second bet is

$$W_0[2pu + 1 - u]2pu + W_0[2pu + 1 - u](1 - u)$$
$$= W_0[2pu + 1 - u]^2$$

For n bets one has $\mathbb{E}[W_n] = W_0(2pu + 1 - u)^n$. Obviously, this expression is growing with u (recall, $p > 0.5$ thus $2p > 1$). Thus in order to maximize the expected terminal wealth a gambler should put at stake all his capital by each bet. However, this is too risky because each bet looms the danger to lose everything and as the number n of bets gets larger and larger a gambler *will* eventually go bankrupt (recall Q10 from the quiz). Thus – if the winnings are *re-invested* - the idea to maximize the expected terminal wealth is actually bad and our gambler needs another approach. On the other hand if he bets nothing (i.e. lets u = 0) he will make no use of his edge. So the optimal fraction is somewhere between zero and one, but where?!

As an alternative to the maximization of the expected terminal wealth, Kelly suggested to maximize the *expected growth rate* (recall Q5 and Q7). Indeed, one can make an outstanding series of returns, say 20%, 30% and 80%, which corresponds to a total return of (1+0.2)(1+0.3)(1+0.8) - 1 = 184%!
But then one may have a bad luck and get a return of -70%. Then the total return will be -34.48% (recall Q5)! In this sense the

maximization of the expected growth rate means that we limit the aftermath of severe negative returns, because just one such negative return can drastically reduce our wealth. At the same time we sufficiently participate in positive returns. Thus in the long run Kelly's approach beats *any other* approach!

As you may have noted, in case of re-investment of winnings the wealth grows exponentially in time, i.e. the time (or the number of investment periods) stays in the exponent (recall formula 1-A6-1). Thus the maximization of the expected growth rate actually means the *maximization of expected logarithmic terminal wealth* $\ln(W_n)$. If we hold an asset for n periods for which the returns are random than we have

$$W_n = W_0 \cdot (1 + r_1) \cdot (1 + r_2) \cdot \ldots \cdot (1 + r_n)$$

Taking logarithm we turn this product into a sum and maximize

$$\mathbb{E}[\ln(1 + r_1) + \ln(1 + r_2) + \ldots + \ln(1 + r_n)]$$

A reader, who is familiar with utility functions, will readily ask whether we just maximize the logarithmic utility. In a sense, yes, and Kelly did recognize this aspect of his approach. But he always pointed at the fact that his argumentation has nothing to do with utility functions and this connection to the logarithmic utility is just a coincidence. However, it is a very happy coincidence! First of all because the logarithmic utility is *myopic*[22]. That is, though we have many bets (or investment periods), we need to act by each bet as *if it were the last one*! Normally, this is not the case and one optimizes running backwards[23]. Indeed, as Elena Wenzel explains, why should we optimize the first step when the second step takes

---

[22] Logarithmic utility has many other nice properties. In general, some utility functions (first of all the logarithmic and negative power utility) are much more useful than the others. Unfortunately, the textbooks on economics usually consider the utility functions very superficially, so that the students get a wrong impression that utility functions is a nice theoretical concept, which is, however, useless in practice.

[23] This approach was introduced by Richard Bellman(1920 - 1984), who called it dynamic programming. By that time the words "computers" and "programming" were the buzz words and Bellman made use of it in order to obtain a grant for his research.

us – directly or figuratively – in a swamp?! That's why we should rather trace our route backward from destination to the start and optimize iteratively. For this we need to know all possible routes and the number of steps. However, in case of an [active] wealth management we usually do not know how many trades we will commit. But in case of acting according to the Kelly criterion we simply do not need to know it! We just optimize every trade as if it were the last one!

Moreover, under fairly general conditions the Kelly criterion maximizes the *median*[24] of the terminal wealth. As a measure of central tendency, the median is often preferred to the expectation. Indeed, assume we need to sum up with a single number the information about the wealth of a group of five people (such as an owner of a company and his employees). If a business owner earns $1000000 per year but pays his employees relatively modest annual salaries of $30000, $40000, $50000 and $60000 then the mean (or "expected" income) is $236000 but the median is $50000, which is obviously much more representative.

Now let us consider the following example[25]: assume there is a stock[26] that yields for each dollar invested, $2.70 or only $0.30, both with probability 1/2. According to the definition 1.1 this is a perfect investment opportunity: the expected wealth is $0.5 \cdot (2.7 + 0.3) = 1.5$, i.e. the expected return is 50%! So far, so good and it does not seem implausible to invest all our capital in

---

[24] Ethier, S. N. (2004). The Kelly system maximizes median fortune. Journal of Applied Probability, 41(5):1230 – 1236

[25] It is Samuelson's example. Paul Samuelson (1915 - 2009) was a Nobel Prize winner in economics and the main critic of Kelly criterion, see "The "fallacy" of maximizing the geometric mean in long sequences of investing or gambling". Proceedings of the National Academy of Sciences, 68(10), 2493-2496). In this sense, it is especially interesting to beat such a prominent critic with his own example. Samuelson actually imposed a constraint either to invest in stock *completely* or not at all. But who can impose such constraint to a trader in a free society and a liberal market?!

[26] And there *are* suchlike stocks, e.g. Nokia (FI0009000681)

this stock. But look what happens in the long run! Since the probabilities to go up and down are equal, we can expect that the number of ups and downs will be approximately equal. Recall our example with 100 coin tosses, it is completely analogous: if we hold this stock for 100 investment periods, the probability that the number of downs remains between 40 and 60 is more than 95%. By 100 trades and a typical 50/50 scenario we yield $[(0.3)(2.7)]^{50} = [0.81]^{50} \approx 0$, i.e. we are broke! In order to make a profit we need at least 55 ups: $(0.3)^{45} \cdot (2.7)^{55} = 1.56842$. But the probability to get 55 or more ups is just 18.41% (check it with R analogously to R-Code 1.1)! Respectively, the probability to make loss is 81.59%, which is too much for a typical risk-averse investor.

But look what happens if we always hold exactly 42% of our wealth in stock and the rest in cash. It means that after each trade we sell a part of stocks if they went up and buy if they went down so that by each trade the wealth fraction invested in stock remains 42%. In this case we yield by a typical scenario

$$([\underbrace{(1-0.42)}_{\text{in cash}} + 2.7 \cdot \underbrace{(0.42)}_{\text{in stock}}][\underbrace{(1-0.42)}_{\text{in cash}} + 0.3 \cdot \underbrace{(0.42)}_{\text{in stock}}])^{50} =$$

$$[(1+1.7\cdot0.42)(1-0.7\cdot0.42)]^{50} = [(1.714)\cdot(0.706)]^{50} = 13828.53$$

What an improvement just by means of a clever money management! Moreover, even if we encounter the worst of the typical scenarios, i.e. just 40 ups and 60 downs we still make profit since $(1.714)^{40} \cdot (0.706)^{60} = 1.94$. That is, with probability of more than 95% we do make profit!

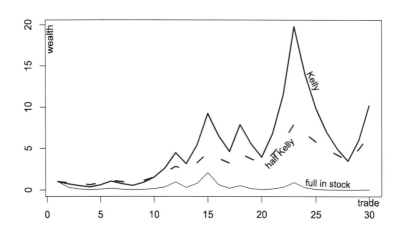

```
install.packages("tseries")
library(tseries)
N_TRADES = 30
outcomes = rbinom(N_TRADES, 1, 0.5)
wealth = array(1.0, dim=N_TRADES)
wealthKelly = array(1.0, dim=N_TRADES)
wealthHalfKelly = array(1.0, dim=N_TRADES)
for( i in 2:(length(outcomes)) )
{
 if(outcomes[i] == 0) {
   wealth[i] = wealth[i-1] * (1 - 0.7)
   wealthKelly[i] = wealthKelly[i-1] * 0.42 *
   (1 - 0.7) + wealthKelly[i-1] * (1 - 0.42)

   wealthHalfKelly[i] = wealthHalfKelly[i-1] * 0.21 *
   (1 - 0.7) + wealthHalfKelly[i-1] * (1 - 0.21)
 }
 else {
   wealth[i] = wealth[i-1] * (1 + 1.7)
   wealthKelly[i] = wealthKelly[i-1] * 0.42 *
   (1 + 1.7) + wealthKelly[i-1] * (1 - 0.42)

   wealthHalfKelly[i] = wealthHalfKelly[i-1] * 0.21 *
   (1 + 1.7) + wealthHalfKelly[i-1] * (1 - 0.21)
 }
}
```

```
chartYmin = min(c(wealth, wealthKelly, wealthHalfKelly))
chartYmax = max(c(wealth, wealthKelly, wealthHalfKelly))
ts.plot(wealth, lwd=1, ylim=c(chartYmin, chartYmax))
lines(wealthKelly, lwd=2,)
lines(wealthHalfKelly, lty=2, lwd=2)
```

Figure 2.1 Kelly, half-Kelly and full investment after 30 trades (a sample scenario).

The constant fraction of 42% is nothing else but the optimal solution according to the Kelly criterion! Since the logarithmic utility is myopic, it suffices to consider a single trade. So we need to maximize

$$0.5\ln(1 + 1.7u) + 0.5\ln(1 - 0.7u)$$

It is $u = 0.42$ that maximizes this expression. You can check it analytically if you have a working knowledge of calculus. Or, alternatively, we can find it numerically with R.

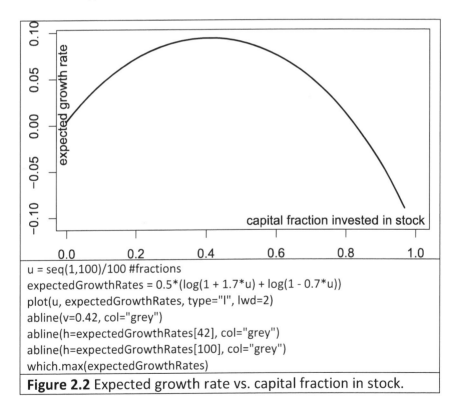

```
u = seq(1,100)/100 #fractions
expectedGrowthRates = 0.5*(log(1 + 1.7*u) + log(1 - 0.7*u))
plot(u, expectedGrowthRates, type="l", lwd=2)
abline(v=0.42, col="grey")
abline(h=expectedGrowthRates[42], col="grey")
abline(h=expectedGrowthRates[100], col="grey")
which.max(expectedGrowthRates)
```

Figure 2.2 Expected growth rate vs. capital fraction in stock.

But looking at figure 2.1 you will probably say that even Kelly strategy is too risky: though the terminal wealth is good the intermediate drop from 20 to 4 (i.e. the drawdown of -80%) is not acceptable. In this case you should reduce the optimal fraction; a common practice is to halve it. This is so called half-Kelly strategy. Though its terminal performance is not as good as Kelly's (asymptotically Kelly beats *any* other strategy) but it is much less risky. Look at figure 2.2! You see that if you bet less or more than the optimal Kelly fraction, your expected growth rate decreases. So if you underbet, you decrease both expected growth rate *and* risk. But if you overbet, the growth rate decreases but the risk grows! Since in practice we can only approximately estimate the optimal Kelly fraction (recall the case "genuine probability vs. its empirical estimate"), we would better underbet. This is also the reason why the half-Kelly strategy is so popular among practitioners.

We see that in Samuelson's example the *maximum* possible expected growth rate is about 9.5%. It tells us what we can, *in principle,* "squeeze" from this investment opportunity in the long term[27]. Actually, such growth rate is not bad (it is better than by DAX) but it would not even double your wealth in five years (recall Q7).

Thus never believe books or people that promise to make you millionaire. I do not affirm that it is principally impossible to turn a couple [of thousands] of bucks into millions. Sometimes it happens, as for instance James "RevShark" DePorre describes in his book "Invest Like a Shark: How a Deaf Guy with No Job and Limited Capital Made a Fortune Investing in the Stock Market". The trick is that Mr. DePorre was lucky to invest in vastly trending markets. Actually, he bought bubbles and sold them at the right time. Currently, he offers wealth management according to his "Sharkfolio" strategy. In this sense I say: I believe he did indeed

---

[27] Completely analogous to the information theory, which tells an engineer what he can, in principle, squeeze from his communication device!

make several millions from $30000 but I do not believe he will reproduce this success with his "Sharkfolio" in the long term.

Once again: the beauty and usefulness of the Kelly criterion is that it lets you estimate what you can *realistically* expect in the *long* term. Can one beat Kelly in short run?! Oh, yes[28]! But in the short run (or more precisely with a small number of trades or investment periods) it is rather a lottery than a systematic investment. Recall, it makes little sense to speak about the expectation by a single coin toss but if you toss a coin 100 times, the number of heads and tails will be quite close to the expected value. The same holds for trading and investment: if you do have an edge, you will profit from it in the long term. But in the short term the randomness dominates and what you get is more a matter of chance.

In this sense, I highly recommend you to read the book "What I have learnt losing a million dollars" by Jim Paul (former governor of the Chicago Mercantile Exchange). It is a rare book, which also sells a bitter truth rather than an [unrealistic] hope. The leitmotiv of this book is that the author got used to breaking the rules and succeeded for a while. But once he failed ... and lost everything. Does it not resemble the cases that we have considered: to lose most of your wealth it suffices to get a severe negative return *just once*, if you overbet. But if you follow the rules, i.e. bet optimally, even a severe negative return will not make you bankrupt.

You are probably wondering, how we can apply Kelly criterion to the stock market. Finally, the stock trading is not coin tossing and there are not just two possible outcomes like heads and tails but much, much more. This is of course true but surprisingly a continuum of outcomes by stock trading can be very well approximated by a simple model á la coin toss.

---

[28] For the technical details have a look at Browne, S.(2000) Can you do better than Kelly in the short run? (Available at: http://www.sbrisk.com/Browne/beat_kelly.pdf)

In order to release the superiority of the Kelly criterion we need a lot or trades (or bets) and the reinvestment of winnings. The latter is very important and probably makes the main difference between gambling and investment. Indeed, according to the Kelly criterion we invest a constant[29] *fraction* of our capital, e.g. 42% as in the case above. But if we play poker with friends or roulette in casino, we usually put a constant *amount* of money at stake, say, $10. In this case, if we have an edge, the capital grows not exponentially but linearly thus it is plausible to optimize the expected terminal wealth.

I, for one, do not play roulette since it is unfavorable game due to the [double] zero. Nor do I play poker. But sometimes I buy out-of-the-money options[30]. Such options, when carefully selected, may be considered as roulette with a positive expectation. The chance to lose everything is still big but there are also some chances to yield a lot of money. My monthly pocket money budget is about €100 but I usually have no time to spend it ☺. On the other hand I sometimes buy a pretty expensive toy, say, a new accessory for my computer. Thus if I invest my pocket money in options and make on average €40 per trade, I yield 12*€40 = €480 to the end of year, which is enough for e.g. an additional monitor (I have four at home). Within the year there are months when I lose my pocket money. If I made profit in previous months, I can compensate my losses with it. But even if I started the year with losses, it is completely no problem for me to refrain from going to a restaurant or bar during the first couple of months. Important is just to get profit to the end of year. But I never confuse gambling with my pocket money and the investment!

---

[29] If the odds change from trade to trade, the optimal Kelly fraction also changes respectively.

[30] In Germany the options, sold to retail investors, are usually called Optionscheine. But they are essentially options, i.e. the rights but not obligations to buy (call option) or sell (put option) an underlying at a given price (strike). The most of Optionscheine are American, i.e. one can exercise them any time before expiry date. Most of traders do not execute but simply sell them (s. Chapter 6).

Chapter 3: More on R, probability, drift and volatility

In previous chapters we have done a minimally sufficient preparation to get started with investment decisions. In this chapter we will make the first concrete steps, recall more facts from probability theory (in particular the normal distribution) and apply Kelly criterion to a univariate portfolio with some capital in ETF on DAX and the rest in cash. We will also extensively use R. Last but not least we will learn (or recall) some practical tips, which are usually not to be found in (text)books but are essential for a practitioner.

First of all let us get some historical data on DAX. Yahoo Finance is an excellent place to start with. You can go directly to http://finance.yahoo.com and download the data you are interested in. The data come in csv-format that can be opened in Excel or read in R. However, there is an even more straightforward way

```
install.packages("quantmod") #do it only by the 1st run
library(quantmod)
getSymbols("^GDAXI", from="1900-01-01")
daxClose = Cl(GDAXI)
daxReturns = ROC(daxClose, type="discrete")
par(mfrow=c(2,1))
plot(daxClose)
plot(daxReturns)
```
R-code 3.1 Getting and plotting data on DAX

After running R-code 3.1 you will see something like figure 3.1. Let us discuss it in detail. The line install.packages("quantmod") installs the package "quantmod" for the quantitative investment analysis[31]. The installation must be done only once, thus we will not call this command anymore in further R-scripts.

---

[31] http://www.quantmod.com. In particular, have a look at a very impressive gallery of screenshots: http://www.quantmod.com/gallery

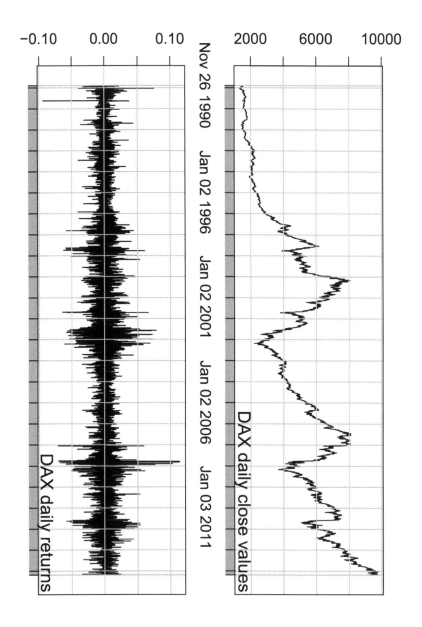

Figure 3.1 DAX daily close values and returns from 1990 to 2014

The line library(quantmod) loads the package "quantmod" in R and should be called every time you are going to use quantmod. We have already encountered suchlike library call for the package "tseries"[32] at figure 2.2. The next command getSymbols("^GDAXI", from="1900-01-01") tells quantmod to load the DAX historical data. By default the data will be loaded from Yahoo Finance. Alternatively, they could be loaded from Google Finance. "^GDAXI" is the ticker for DAX. In order to load the data by means of quantmod you need to know a ticker, which you can always find by Yahoo Finance (just search for "DAX" at http://finance.yahoo.com).

Note that in general, there are several tickers for an asset. For example, RWE.DE means RWE stock data on Xetra and RWE.F means RWE stock data on Frankfurter Börse[33].

We request R to get the data from 01.01.1900 but, as you can see at figure 3.1, Yahoo provides the data only from 26.11.1990. However, it is sufficient for practical purposes[34]. The next line daxClose = Cl(GDAXI) extracts the close prices from the downloaded data. The data contain the daily OHLC (Open-High-Low-Close) prices and sometimes the trade volume.

The close prices are considered the most significant and representative since they are calculated at the end of day[35] and thus reflect the influence of all market agents.

---

[32] tseries: Time series analysis and computational finance
http://cran.r-project.org/web/packages/tseries/index.html
[33] RWE is a large German energy company. Xetra is the most important electronic trading platform in Germany. Frankfurter Börse (Frankfurt Stock Exchange) is the oldest exchange in Germany.
[34] You may still need earlier data if you want e.g. to analyze the stock dynamics during the Black Monday Crisis (1987) or even during the Great Depression. For example, as the global financial crisis in 2008 broke out, I wanted to have a closer look at the historical data on US stocks for 1929-1932. Yahoo Finance or Google Finance cannot usually help in this case but Yahoo or Google themselves can ☺.
[35] Some financial institutions consider 11:00 a.m. prices instead. However, they are generally not available for an individual investor.

The command `daxReturns = ROC(daxClose, type="discrete")` means to calculate the returns from DAX daily close values. We specify a parameter "type" as "discrete" to calculate the simple returns; otherwise the logarithmic returns would be calculated by default. The command `par(mfrow=c(2,1))` splits the graphical window of R in two horizontal panels and the last two lines plot the graphs[36]. Note that quantmod formats its data object in such a way that the R-command "plot" draws it nicely.

Now let us analyze what we see at figure 3.1. At first look at the DAX close values. We immediately see two crises: the first flop in 2003 (the dotcom crisis) and the second in March 2009 (global financial crisis). Interestingly, the drawdown by the dotcom crisis was stronger, though this crisis was much milder than the global financial crisis. Probably by the time of the dotcom crisis nobody believed that DAX will grow to 8000 points again. Or probably the resoluteness of the USA and European Union to mitigate the global financial crisis played its role in 2009. There is also a significant correction in 2011 due to the downgrade of US credit rating from AAA to AA+ by S&P. In my opinion there was not only psychological shock but also a structural shift. As a matter of fact most financial institutions are obliged by the regulators to have their risks limited. Or, more precisely, to assure that the VaR[37] (which comes from a risk model) is kept below some limit. The downgrade of the US government bonds to AA+ has automatically made many portfolios more risky, so the institutions had to get rid of a part of the most risky assets in order to keep the VaR acceptable.

We also see the distinct periods of the up- and down-trend. They are especially distinct since the figure 3.1 depicts a relatively long time span in a small scale. Had we magnified the chart, we would see more and more irregularities (that cancel out as time goes by). In particular, it means that an investor can be passive during sufficiently long time periods and simply let his profit grow. All he

---

[36] What you see at Figure 3.1 is a slightly modified output of R-code 3.1.

[37] Value-at-Risk. Probably not the best but definitely the most common risk measure by financial institutions.

needs to do is "merely" to choose the right entry and exit points. This problem is far from being trivial but is also not unsolvable. At least the exit points are more or less clear from the chart: before the up-trend bends one can usually observe a period of stagnation. Of course an investor should not just read the chart. Rather he should permanently stay informed about the national and world economies, new trends (like dotcoms or renewable energy) and so on.

Next, look at the chart of the DAX daily returns. First of all you probably see that contrary to the previous chart with clear up- and down-trends there is no suchlike regularity. Rather the positive and the negative returns alternate chaotically. However, there is another pattern: sometimes the amplitude of returns is small (about ±2% per day) and sometimes it is more than ±5% per day. In other words there are the periods of high and low volatility[38]. Moreover, if you collate both charts, you will see that the periods of low volatility correspond to the up-trends, whereas in the case of the down-trends the volatility is higher and takes its maximum as the index reaches its bottom.

So let us try to formalize our observations in terms of a (simple) mathematical model. First of all the chaotic alternation of the returns lets us assume that the returns are serially independent. Just like in case of a symmetric coin: if we know the outcomes of the previous 100 or even 1000 tosses, it does not give us any information on what we could get by the next toss. It may be a pity for a speculator but for a mathematician a sequence of the *independent* random variables (i.e. of daily returns in our case) is very pleasing because it is easy to model. In the chapter on backtesting we will formally check whether this assumption is true but so far please take for granted that it usually is. The next feature, which a mathematician wishes to have, is the *identical probability distribution* of returns. When we toss a coin, it does not change its properties (we assume that a coin remains intact after falling on the

---

[38] This stylized fact is usually called volatility clustering.

floor). Thus the probabilities of all events - in this simplest case of heads and tails - do not change from toss to toss. For the asset returns it is definitely not true alone due to the volatility clustering. However, for a relatively small time span the volatility may probably remain more or less constant, at least at a first approximation[39]. Finally, we may assume that the returns are *normally* distributed. Normal (a.k.a. Gaussian) distribution fails to capture many stylized facts of current turbulent financial markets. However, it allows to build a very elegant model, which can be easily[40] refined for practical usage. The best property of the normal distribution is as follows: a sum of random variables - *not even necessarily independent and identically distributed* - usually converges to the normal distribution. This is known as the *Central Limit Theorem* (CLT). But "usually" does not mean "always" and in particular the convergence fails when a panic breaks out in the market and everyone sells[41]. But during the calm periods someone buys, someone sells and everyone is relatively small compared to the whole market. This suffices for the normality of returns, at least theoretically.

Formally, a random variable $\mathbb{X}$ is normally distributed if its *probability density* is defined as follows:

---

[39] In the transient points, e.g. in which a crisis occurs, it is not the case even to a first approximation.

[40] A current trend in theoretical mathematical finance is to invent more and more complicated models so that eventually nobody can calibrate them to the real data or even understand. We will avoid this vicious way, adding complexity only if it brings more usefulness than troubles.

[41] For the modeling of a long term investment it is not too critical. Although during a crisis the returns are definitely non-normal, this effect will be "absorbed" in the long run. The CLT holds again since the terminal wealth is determined by many intermediary returns (although there are some nuances: because the returns influence the terminal wealth multiplicatively, the latter converges to the *log*-normal distribution).
Including a non-normal component in the model will likely help to simulate the maximum drawdown more precisely but will hardly improve the modeling precision of the terminal wealth distribution. Additionally, the model will become [much] more complicated.

$$f(x|\mu, \sigma) = \frac{1}{\sigma\sqrt{2\pi}} e^{-\frac{(x-\mu)^2}{2\sigma^2}}$$

Formula 3.1 The density of the normal distribution

The parameters μ and σ are arbitrary but fixed. The formula 3.1 gives us the probability that (given μ and σ) the random variable $\mathbb{X}$ gets a value in an infinitesimal interval containing x. Informally, we can say that this is just the probability to get $\mathbb{X} = x$. But mathematically it is not correct since the probability of this event is zero. Indeed, the probabilities of all events must sum to 1 thus we can define the (nonzero) probabilities of events like $\mathbb{X} = x$ only for a *finite* number of points. But there is a continuum of points on the number axes! In order to circumvent this problem, the mathematicians consider the events like $\mathbb{X} \leq x$ rather than $\mathbb{X} = x$. The probabilities of such events are calculated by a *cumulative distribution function*. For the normal distribution it is

$$\mathbb{P}(\mathbb{X} \leq x) = \int_{-\infty}^{x} \frac{1}{\sigma\sqrt{2\pi}} e^{-\frac{(x-\mu)^2}{2\sigma^2}} dx$$

Formula 3.2 The cumulative distribution function of the normal distribution

The integral on the right-hand side can*not* be calculated in closed form. But of course it can be calculated numerically as precisely as we want. Analogously to the definitions 1.1 and 1.2 we can calculate the expectation and the variance of a continuously distributed random variable. However, we need to replace the sum with integral. It turns out, that for the normal distribution these integrals have closed form solutions and the parameters μ and σ are just the expectation and the variance!

$$\mathbb{E}[\mathbb{X}] := \int_{-\infty}^{\infty} x f(x) dx$$

Definition 3.1 The expectation of a continuous random variable

$$\mathbb{VAR}[\mathbb{X}] := \int_{-\infty}^{\infty} (x - \mathbb{E}[\mathbb{X}])^2 f(x) dx$$

Definition 3.2 The variance of a continuous random variable

where $f(x)$ is the probability density function.

As to the standard deviation, the definition 1.3 remains unchanged: the standard deviation is still the square root of the variance.
In particular for the normal distribution it holds

$$\mathbb{E}[\mathbb{X}] = \int_{-\infty}^{\infty} x \frac{1}{\sigma\sqrt{2\pi}} e^{-\frac{(x-\mu)^2}{2\sigma^2}} dx = \mu$$

Formula 3.3 Expectation of a normally distributed random variable

$$\mathbb{VAR}[\mathbb{X}] = \int_{-\infty}^{\infty} (x - \mu)^2 \frac{1}{\sigma\sqrt{2\pi}} e^{-\frac{(x-\mu)^2}{2\sigma^2}} dx = \sigma^2$$

Formula 3.4 Variance of a normally distributed random variable

As you can readily see the normal distribution is completely and uniquely defined by its expectation and variance, or in other words,

38

by its first two central statistical moments. For other continuous probability distributions it is not the case. However, the first two moments will suffice for the rest of the book. Additionally, we may have included in our model the probability of a crash as follows: let $r := \lambda \mathbb{X} + (1 - \lambda)\mathbb{D}$ where r is a DAX return, $\mathbb{X}$ is a normally distributed random variable, $\mathbb{D}$ is a dropdown amplitude (which can be random as well) and λ is a binomially distributed random variable, which takes values in either 0 or 1. This is a so-called *mixture distribution*; the value of return is now determined by more than one random variable. However, the calibration of the mixture distribution parameters is beyond the scope of this book and we do not really need it in case of a long term investment, since the dropdown component will all the same be absorbed due to the CLT.

If you are confused by the formulas and integrals, do not worry too much. I mean, if you do learn this stuff, it will be very helpful. But if not, just keep in mind that one can always *discretize* the probability density of a continuous random variable. And we do not need [very] complicated formulas in order to deal with discrete random variables. Last but not least, we always have R at hand ☺! Let us have a look at the interrelation of the binomial and normal distributions. At figure 3.2 we plot the histogram of the binomial distribution with 10 trials (coin tosses) and the probability of success (this is probability to get a head) equal to 0.55 Further we estimate the expectation and the standard deviation of this distribution by R-commands mean(coinTosses) and sd(coinTosses) and draw the density of the normal distribution with these parameters. As you see, it fits nicely to the histogram. Thus if you are confused with the normal distribution, you can comprehend it in terms of the binomial distribution.

Even more similarity is visible at figure 3.3, where we plot the densities of the binomial distribution and the normal distribution with the same mean and variance. You may wonder how a binomial distribution, which is discrete, can have a continuous density function. Well, just like we can discretize any continuous function, we can "continualize" a discrete function. The theory of "continualizing" is complicated (so-called kernel smoothing) but do

not worry, the R-command [density(coinTosses)] will do everything
for you. Just note that a kernel smoother is, in a sense, a more
efficient aggregation method than a histogram. And that is what
you see: the densities at figure 3.3 are much closer to each other
than the density and the histogram at figure 3.2.

Now we corroborate the statement that we can, in principle,
comprehend the markets in terms of the coin tosses. First of all,
there are many traders on the market. As long as there is neither
panic nor gold-rush, some traders sell, some buy. But this is
essentially a binomial distribution: we just say "buy and sell" instead
of "head and tail".

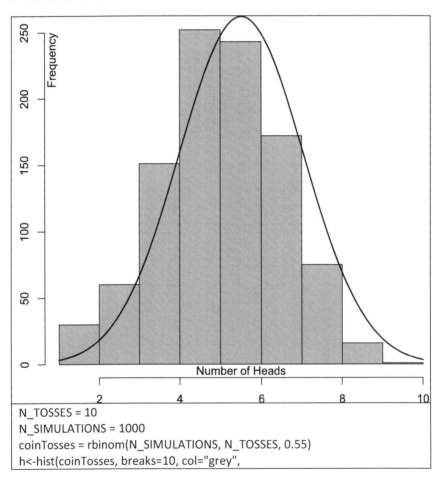

```
N_TOSSES = 10
N_SIMULATIONS = 1000
coinTosses = rbinom(N_SIMULATIONS, N_TOSSES, 0.55)
h<-hist(coinTosses, breaks=10, col="grey",
```

```
    xlab="Number of Heads",
      main="Histogram with Normal Curve")
  xfit<-seq(min(coinTosses),max(coinTosses),length=1000)
  yfit<-dnorm(xfit,mean=mean(coinTosses),sd=sd(coinTosses))
  yfit <- yfit*diff(h$mids[1:2])*length(coinTosses)
  lines(xfit, yfit, col="black", lwd=2)
```

Figure 3.2 Interrelation of binomial and normal distributions[42]

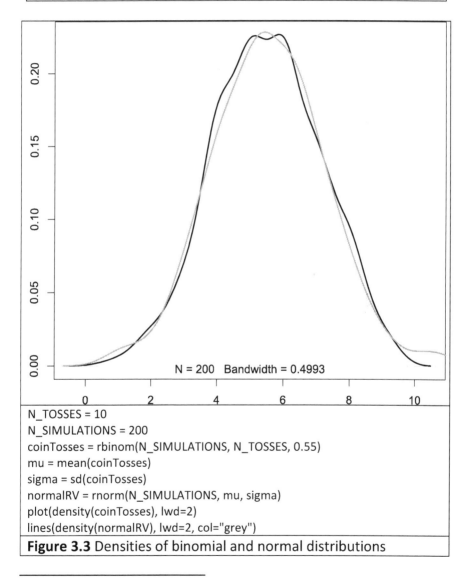

N = 200   Bandwidth = 0.4993

```
N_TOSSES = 10
N_SIMULATIONS = 200
coinTosses = rbinom(N_SIMULATIONS, N_TOSSES, 0.55)
mu = mean(coinTosses)
sigma = sd(coinTosses)
normalRV = rnorm(N_SIMULATIONS, mu, sigma)
plot(density(coinTosses), lwd=2)
lines(density(normalRV), lwd=2, col="grey")
```

Figure 3.3 Densities of binomial and normal distributions

---

[42] R-Code partly borrowed from http://statmethods.net/graphs/density.html

In a bull market there are more buyers and in a bear market more sellers. We can reflect this via the probability of success of a binomial distribution. We have seen that even by 10 coin tosses the binomial distribution converges to normal. In market terms it would mean that if an asset is traded by at least 10 independent traders that have a similar capital, the asset returns will be normally distributed. In reality, there are thousands of traders.

Enough theory, let us check whether the DAX returns are normally distributed. At first we start with daily returns (recall figure 3.1). To proceed we run the following R-code (compare it to R-code 3.1)

```
#get data
library(quantmod)
getSymbols("^GDAXI", from="1900-01-01")
daxClose = Cl(GDAXI)
daxReturns = ROC(daxClose, type="discrete")

#qqplot + return density and normal density together
n = length(daxReturns)
mu = mean(daxReturns[2:n]) #first array value is NA, drop it!
sigma = sd(daxReturns[2:n])
normalRets = rnorm((n-1), mu, sigma)
par(mfrow=c(2,1))
plot(density(daxReturns[2:n]), lwd=2)
lines(density(normalRets), lwd=2, col="grey")
qqnorm(daxReturns[2:n])
```
R-code 3.2a Checking DAX daily returns for normality

We are going to discuss this code in detail. The lines beginning with # are just comments.

It is very useful to comment your code! If you don't then even you, yourself, may not be able to understand your own code in several months.

You can write comments both in a separate line or at the end of any line (after an R-command).

The first four commands are the same as in R-code 3.1. However, there is no line install.packages("quantmod"). A package must be installed only once, and you have already done it as you ran R-code 3.1.

The line $\boxed{n = length(daxReturns)}$ counts the number of elements in array "daxReturns". The first element of this array is set to "NA" (non-applicable). As a matter of fact, if there is a time series of *n* asset prices, there can be at most *n-1* returns. But for some reason the author of quantmod decided to keep the lengths of array of prices and of array of returns equal to each other. Thus we should drop the first element of the array "daxReturns", otherwise we will get an error message from R. The line $\boxed{daxReturns[2:n]}$ just means "take all elements of daxReturns from the 2nd to the last one". The commands $\boxed{mean}$ and $\boxed{sd}$ calculate the (empirical) mean and the standard deviation of an array. The larger is the array (i.e. the sample of observed data), the closer are the estimated *mu* and *sigma* to their genuine counterparts.

With command $\boxed{normalRets = rnorm((n-1), mu, sigma)}$ we sample *n-1* elements from a normal distribution with parameters *mu* and *sigma*. We have enough empirical data (when I wrote this chapter *n* was 5906, i.e. there were available 5905 historical daily returns). Respectively, the *mu* and the *sigma* can be estimated with a pretty good precision. Thus if the daily DAX returns are normally distributed, the densities of *daxReturns* and of *normalRets* should be nearly the same.

Additionally, we can check whether they agree in *quantiles*. Informally, *q(x)* is the quantile at level *x* if *q(x)* is the smallest element of a sample such that *x·100%* of elements of this sample are not larger than *q(x)*. For example, for an (ordered) sample {1,2,5,7,10,10,12,14,20,31} we have *q(0.9)=20* since 90% of the elements are smaller than or equal to 20. Analogously *q(0.4) = 7*. And formally, the quantile function is the (generalized[43]) inverse of

---

[43] At first glance it is unclear how to define, e.g. *q(0.05)* or *q(0.67)* since we have only 10 values. Also it is unclear how to define *q(0.5)*, since 40% of the values are less than or equal to 7 but 60% of the values are not larger than 10 and there is

the cumulative distribution function. In our example (given the probabilities of all ten outcomes are equal[44]) $P(X \leq 7) = 0.4$ and $P(X \leq 20) = 0.9$. Note that the *median* is nothing else but $q(0.5)$

Two samples drawn from the same probability distribution should ideally agree at all quantiles. The command qqnorm(daxReturns[2:n]) plots the quantiles of the DAX returns against the quantiles of the [standard[45]] normal distribution. Ideally, the qqplot should be a straight line.

Finally, the command par(mfrow=c(2,1)) means to split the graphical window of R in two parts. In the first window the qqplot will be plotted. In the second window we at first plot the density of the DAX returns: plot(density(daxReturns[2:n]), lwd=2) where *lwd=2* makes line thicker. Additionally, we want to sketch the density of the normal distribution at the same plot. But each time we call "plot"-command, it clears its graphic window. Thus we call the "lines"-command instead. Additionally, we tell R to draw the normal density in grey, which makes the plot more legible.

Both qqplot and visual comparison of the density functions are informal methods. But the practitioners really like them, esp. the qqplot. As you see, the daily DAX returns are hardly normal and the main problem is the heavy tails of the empirical DAX returns. You know that the density of the normal distribution is defined for the whole real line, i.e. infinite, or anyway large absolute values of returns are theoretically possible. However, in case of the normal distribution they rarely occur.

---

no value between 7 and 10. Introducing the generalized inverse solves these (and not only these) problems. However, it is rather relevant for a theoretical consistency than for the practical applications.

[44] For a *raw* empirical sample this assumption is nearly always made. Of course the probability of 10 is likely larger than of any other value since 10 appeared twice. One takes this fact into account when one makes a histogram or density function from a raw empirical sample. But in a raw sample (i.e. just recorded, probably ordered but not aggregated values) these two 10's are considered as separate events.

[45] I.e. with $\mu = 0$ and $\sigma = 1$

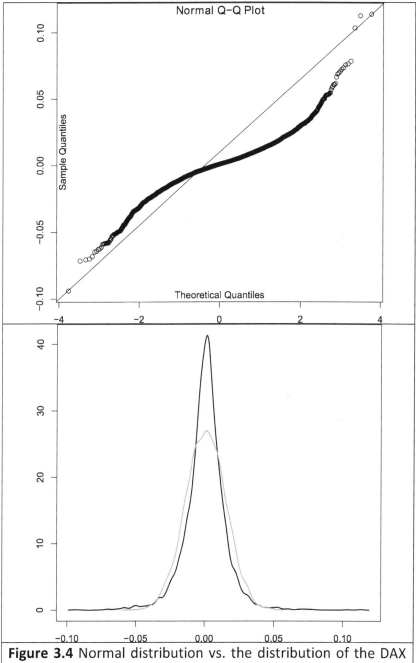

Figure 3.4 Normal distribution vs. the distribution of the DAX daily returns: qqplot and density functions.

One says that the normal distribution has *light tails*, which means that nearly all realizations of a normally distributed random variable will be located around μ (i.e. around the expected value). Outliers are virtually impossible, since the probability of the large deviations decays extremely fast[46]. On the other hand an empirical distribution is a priori finite. However, there are enough days on which the absolute values of returns are very large. Lehman Brothers goes bankrupt and the DAX drops severely or the EU authorities announce EFSF (European Financial Stability Facility) and the DAX jumps high. On such days nearly all traders sell or buy thus the central limit theorem does not work. But it follows that if we drop such days from our sample, then what remains should be normally distributed. Actually, the normal and empirical density functions generally agree in bodies (central parts) and disagree in tails, so let us cut the latter! After you ran the R-code 3.2a, run the R-code 3.2b

```
#... run after running 3.2a otherwise it will not work
cap = 3 * sd(daxReturns[2:n])
capRets = array(0.0, dim=0)
for( i in 2:n )
{
   if( abs(daxReturns[i]) < cap )
   {
      capRets = c(capRets, daxReturns[i])
   }
}
qqnorm(capRets)
print( length(capRets) / length(daxReturns[2:n]) )
```

R-code 3.2b Checking DAX daily returns for normality - tails cut

A well-known fact is that a normally distributed random variable hardly deviates from its expectation by more than ±3 standard deviations. In a for-loop we run through all empirical DAX returns and take only those that suit this $\pm 3\sigma$ criterion. We do not know in advance how many empirical returns will suit. So we first create an

---

[46] You need to know calculus in order to understand why. Alternatively, you may just play with R command "pnorm(x)": plot the values of *x* against *pnorm(x)* to see the speed of decay.

empty array of truncated (or capped) returns
capRets = array(0.0, dim=0) and then append values to it by means
of capRets = c(capRets, daxReturns[i]) .

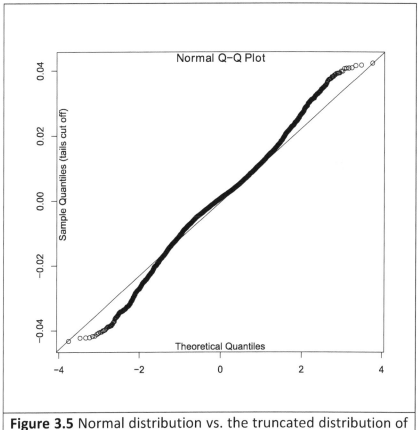

Figure 3.5 Normal distribution vs. the truncated distribution of
the DAX returns

The R-command c stands for concatenate, so at each step, at which
abs(daxReturns[i]) < cap holds true, the new value is appended to
the current values of *capRets*. Note that from the technical point of
view it is very inefficient programming style[47] and you have

---

[47] Because the array must be re-allocated in memory each time the
concatenation occurs. In more efficient programming languages, e.g. in C++,
there is a command push_back, which adds an element to an array (or in terms of
C++ to a vector) without memory re-allocation.

probably noticed that R needs a couple of seconds to run the R-code 3.2b. But on the other hand it is also probably the shortest piece of programming code that does the job.

Finally the line `print( length(capRets) / length(daxReturns[2:n]) )` gives us the fraction of returns that suit the $\pm 3\sigma$ criterion. In my case it was 98.27%.

As you can see at figure 3.5 the quantiles agree much better than at figure 3.4. So under the assumption that no market turbulence will take place we may model the returns with a normal distribution. Of course this assumption must be made with caution; however, you have seen that the probability of the tail events (i.e. the returns that do not suit the $\pm 3\sigma$ criterion) is less than 2%. So for a short term investment (about a month or two) we may assume no market turbulence (unless we expect an announcement of crucial governmental decisions or important macroeconomic statistics in the near future). And as we have already mentioned, in the long term the market turbulence will be absorbed by the CLT. But in the midterm there may be a significant inaccuracy due to the assumption of the return normality. In particular, a [temporary] drawdown may be much more severe than the model predicts.

Now let us have a look whether the monthly returns are normally distributed. Finally, the daily returns are not very relevant for an individual investor: it is unlikely that he has time to trade every day. Rather he would invest for a time span of several months or even years. The monthly returns are determined by a composition of the daily returns thus by CLT the monthly returns might be normal even if the daily returns are not. As usual, let us check this assumption.

```
#... run after running 3.2a otherwise it will not work
daxMonthlyRets = periodReturn(GDAXI, period='monthly')
n = length(daxMonthlyRets)
mu = mean(daxMonthlyRets)
sigma = sd(daxMonthlyRets)
normalRets = rnorm(n, mu, sigma)
par(mfrow=c(3,1))
plot(daxMonthlyRets)
qqnorm(daxMonthlyRets)
plot(density(daxMonthlyRets), lwd=2)
lines(density(normalRets), lwd=2, col="grey")
```

R-code 3.2c Checking DAX monthly returns for normality

(Note that the quantmod-function *periodReturn* returns an array that does not have "NA" as the first element).

Comparing figures 3.4 and 3.7 we assume that the normality assumption is more suitable for the monthly than for the daily returns. The fit is still not perfect and a disagreement in tails is visible as well. This is even though there is a composition of three "averaging" factors that support the CLT, namely:

1. DAX consists of 30 different stocks (the pitfall is, however, that their returns are correlated, sometimes very closely, thus the diversification effect is not so strong)
2. These stocks are very liquid and the trading volume is high
3. A monthly return is determined by 22 daily returns

But as a first approximation, we may still assume that the monthly returns are normally distributed. Note that the asset *returns* (and not the asset *prices*) are modeled by the normal distribution. Normal distribution is symmetric and defined for the whole real line but an asset price cannot fall below zero. Had we worked with continuously compounded interest and logarithmic returns, the stock prices would be *log-normally* distributed. For the daily or monthly simple returns there is no such closed form solution (though also in these cases the asset prices are approximately lognormal). Anyway, we can calculate the distribution of the asset price from the distribution of returns numerically.

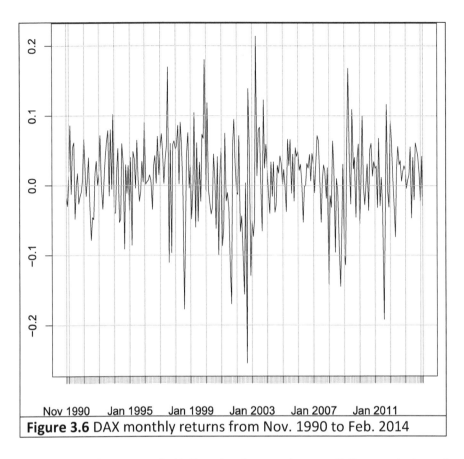

Figure 3.6 DAX monthly returns from Nov. 1990 to Feb. 2014

Now let us apply Kelly criterion to the portfolio consisting of an ETF on DAX and a (riskless) bank account. We assume the normality of the monthly DAX returns and monthly portfolio restructuring. We set the annual riskless interest rate to 3%, which is pretty close to the mean overnight rate for the time span from 1900 to 2014. Then $r = 0.25\%$ is the respective monthly rate. We assume the investment for 10 years = 120 months. Note that though the Kelly criterion is myopic and the number of holding periods does not matter for the formal optimization, in practical terms it becomes superior only in the long run.

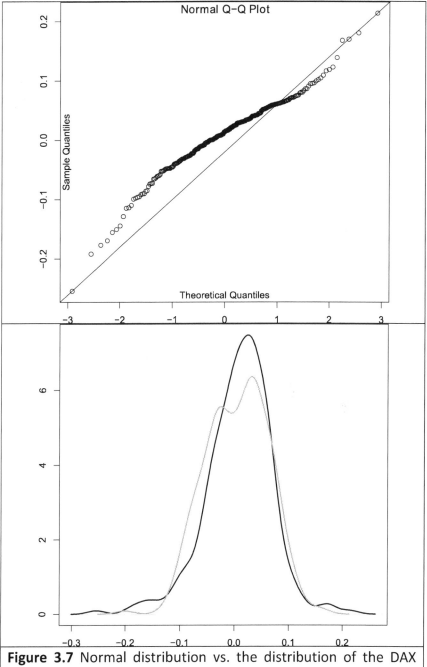

Figure 3.7 Normal distribution vs. the distribution of the DAX monthly returns: qqplot and density functions.

```
mu = 0.0085 #empirical value
sigma = 0.0605 # and this too
N_SIMULATIONS = 10000
N_MONTHS = 120 #10 years investment horizon
simResult = array(1.0, dim=c(N_SIMULATIONS, N_MONTHS))
for( i in 1:N_SIMULATIONS)
{
  rets = rnorm(N_MONTHS, mu, sigma)
  for( k in 2:N_MONTHS )
  {
     simResult[i, k] = simResult[i, (k-1)] * (1+rets[k])
  }
}
par(mfrow=c(2,1))
ts.plot(simResult[1, ], lwd="2")
lines(simResult[1000, ], lwd="2", col="grey")
lines(simResult[5000, ], lwd="2", col="brown")
plot(density(simResult[,N_MONTHS])) #terminal prices
```
R-code 3.2d Simulating DAX in ten years

Without loss of generality we can set the initial wealth to 1. If we keep a wealth fraction u in DAX then at each step the portfolio yields

$$u(1+r_{\text{dax}})+(1-u)(1+r) = u(r_{\text{dax}}-r)+(1+r)$$

Formula 3.5 The yield of a portfolio "DAX + a bank account"

So we are going to find the optimal Kelly fraction as follows:
1. we try iteratively the fractions 1%, 2%, ..., 100% in DAX and the rest in a bank account
2. for each fraction we simulate 1000 scenarios and calculate the mean logarithmic terminal wealth among all scenarios
3. finally, we look which fraction in DAX yields the maximal mean logarithmic terminal wealth (i.e. the maximal expected growth rate).

```
N_SIMULATIONS = 10000
N_MONTHS = 120 #10 years investment horizon
N_STEPS = 100 #iteratively try 1%, 2%, ... , 100% capital in DAX
library(quantmod)

#get data, set or estimate parametes
getSymbols("^GDAXI", from="1900-01-01")
#getSymbols("^GDAXI", from="2007-01-01") #try also this
daxMonthlyRets = periodReturn(GDAXI, period='monthly')
n = length(daxMonthlyRets)
mu = mean(daxMonthlyRets)
sigma = sd(daxMonthlyRets)
r = 0.03 / 12 #monthly return thus divide by 12

#find optimal Kelly fraction
wealth = array(1.0, dim=c(N_STEPS, N_SIMULATIONS))
meanLogWealth = array(0.0, dim=N_STEPS)
for( u in 1:N_STEPS ) {
  for( i in 2:N_SIMULATIONS)
  {
    monRets = rnorm(N_MONTHS, mu, sigma)
    for(m in 1:N_MONTHS)
    {
      if( monRets[m] < -0.99 ) monRets[m] = -0.99 #truncate
      if( monRets[m] > 0.99 ) monRets[m] = 0.99 #at +/-99%

      portfolioRet = ((u / N_STEPS)*(monRets[m] - r) + (1 + r))
      wealth[u, i] = wealth[u, (i-1)] * portfolioRet
    }
  }
  meanLogWealth[u] = mean(log(wealth[u, ]))
}
max(meanLogWealth)
which.max(meanLogWealth)
```

R-code 3.3a Looking for the optimal Kelly fraction

The first part of the R-Code 3.3a is already familiar to you. There is something new in the section marked with "#find optimal Kelly fraction".

Line wealth=array(1.0, dim=c(N_STEPS, N_SIMULATIONS)) declares a two dimensional array (i.e. a matrix with N_STEPS rows and

N_SIMULATIONS columns) and populates all its cells with 1.0. Further there are three nested for-loops. The outer loop comes to the next step only after the inner loop is completely executed. In our case it means that at first u is set to 1, i is set to 2 and m is set to 1 and runs to N_MONTHS (i.e. to 100). Then i is set to 3 and m runs once again from 1 to 100. As soon as i reaches N_SIMULATIONS (i.e. 10000), u will be set to 2. As you can see, the total number of operations is equal to N_STEPS * N_MONTHS * N_SIMULATIONS = 120 millions. That's why R-code 3.3a needs some to time to run.

Also note the line if(monRets[m] < -0.99) monRets[m] = -0.99. As we have already noted, the extreme returns drawn from a normal distribution are rare but not impossible. Thus we need to truncate, otherwise we may get a negative wealth, which does not make sense with no leverage and no short selling constraints. The command meanLogWealth[u] = mean(log(wealth[u,])) is very capacious. First of all wealth[u,] means the u-th row of the matrix wealth, i.e. it is a one-dimensional array with N_SIMULATION elements. The command log(wealth[u,]) means to calculate the logarithm of each element of array wealth[u,], i.e. it returns an array of the same length[48]. Finally, we calculate the mean value of the logarithmic terminal wealth; this is done for each fraction u. The command which.max(meanLogWealth) finds out the position of the maximal element in array meanLogWealth. In my case it was 93, i.e. the numerically calculated optimal Kelly fraction of the capital in DAX is equal to 93%.

There is also a theoretical solution of this optimization problem obtained by Robert C. Merton[49]; the optimal Kelly fraction[50] is calculated by

---

[48] Note that in programming languages like C++ or Java the built-in mathematical functions like log(x) are applicable only to the scalar arguments.

[49] Robert C. Merton (born in 1944) is a Nobel laureate in economics, mostly known for his contribution to the continuous-time stochastic finance. He is also known for his epic failure as a fund manager by the LTCM hedge fund.

[50] As Samuelson's diligent student, Merton, himself, prefers speaking about the maximization of the logarithmic utility and not about the Kelly criterion.

$$u^\star = \frac{\mu - r}{\sigma^2}$$

Formula 3.6 Merton's optimal portfolio for logarithmic utility in continuous time

and in our case is equal to 166%, i.e. we would need to use the leverage. However, his solution is valid for a *continuous-time* model[51], by which the returns are continuously compounded (recall formula 1-A11-1). So the difference of 93% (numeric) vs. 166% (closed form) are not due to the inaccuracy of the numerical computation but rather due to the model difference[52] *and* the sensitivity of the optimization problem to the input parameters.

In either case, this is a clear argument for a passive investment! There is no big difference between 93% and 100% (figure 3.8), so a typical busy and short-of-time investor would just invest 100% and avoid annoying monthly portfolio restructuring. However, this argument holds only for an "ivory tower" investor, i.e. an investor who does not [wish to] follow the news. I mean it is hardly feasible to try to catch each market movement but it is both reasonable and feasible to sell or at least to reduce your portfolio when you get the breaking news like the bankruptcy of Lehman Brothers or expect the downgrade of US rating.

---

[51] For this model, the portfolio value evolves according to the stochastic differential equation $X_t = X_0 \exp\left(\left[r + u(\mu - r) - \frac{1}{2}\sigma^2 u^2\right] t + u\sigma W_t\right)$, where W_t is the Wiener process (a.k.a. the Brownian motion).

[52] You can easily adapt R-code 3.3a to the Merton's model. Just set *N_STEPS = 200* drop all lines containing monRets and replace the line *portfolioRet = ((u / N_STEPS)*(monRets[m] - r) + (1 + r))* with *portfolioRet = exp(r + u/100*(mu-r)- 0.5*(sigma^2)*(u/100)^2 + u/100*sigma*rnorm(1))*

Then you will also get a numerical solution close to 166%.

Additionally, not every investor is ready to bear a severe drawdown of -50% or more. In this case, the fractional Kelly strategies may be attractive. I, for one, would prefer 0.3-Kelly in this case. It triples the wealth by the maximum drawdown of -22%, which I still can tolerate. You should experiment and find the fraction that suits *you*. Remember, however, that even an aggressive investor rarely follows the full Kelly strategy. As a matter of fact, Kelly's approach is pretty sensitive to the parameter estimation. In order to understand it let us make one more computational experiment as in R-code 3.3c.

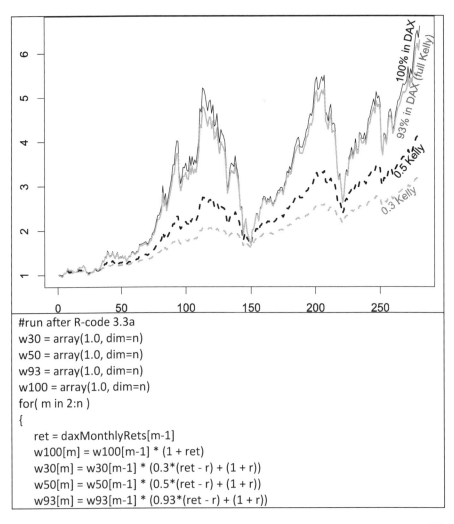

```
#run after R-code 3.3a
w30 = array(1.0, dim=n)
w50 = array(1.0, dim=n)
w93 = array(1.0, dim=n)
w100 = array(1.0, dim=n)
for( m in 2:n )
{
    ret = daxMonthlyRets[m-1]
    w100[m] = w100[m-1] * (1 + ret)
    w30[m] = w30[m-1] * (0.3*(ret - r) + (1 + r))
    w50[m] = w50[m-1] * (0.5*(ret - r) + (1 + r))
    w93[m] = w93[m-1] * (0.93*(ret - r) + (1 + r))
```

```
}
ts.plot(w100)
lines(w30, col="grey", lwd=2, lty=2)
lines(w50, col="black", lwd=2, lty=2)
lines(w93, col="grey", lwd=2)
```

Figure 3.8 and R-code 3.3b DAX + bank account portfolio: 100% in DAX, full Kelly, 0.5-Kelly and 0.3-Kelly fractions. Retrospective analysis for 1990-2014

```
##run after R-code 3.3a
kellySensitivity <-function()
{
#set "genuine" parameters
n = length(daxMonthlyRets)  #281
trueMu = mean(daxMonthlyRets)  #0.008567559
trueSigma = sd(daxMonthlyRets)  #0.06050129

#make three iterations
for( iteration in 1:3 )
{
  #get a limited(!) from the genuine distribution
  rets = rnorm(n, trueMu, trueSigma)
  mu =  mean(rets)
  sigma = sd(rets)

  #find optimal Kelly fraction
  wealth = array(1.0, dim=c(N_STEPS, N_SIMULATIONS))
  meanLogWealth = array(0.0, dim=N_STEPS)
  for( u in 1:N_STEPS )
  {
   for( i in 2:N_SIMULATIONS)
   {
    monRets = rnorm(N_MONTHS, mu, sigma)
    for(m in 1:N_MONTHS)
    {
     if( monRets[m] < -0.99 ) monRets[m] = -0.99 #truncate
     if( monRets[m] >  0.99 ) monRets[m] = 0.99 #at +/-99%

     portfolioRet = ((u / N_STEPS)*(monRets[m] - r) + (1 + r))
     wealth[u, i] = wealth[u, (i-1)] * portfolioRet
    }
   }
   meanLogWealth[u] = mean(log(wealth[u, ]))
```

```
    }
  print(paste("Iteration: ", iteration, sep=""))
  print(max(meanLogWealth))
  print(which.max(meanLogWealth))
  }
}


#compile before running to speed-up
require(compiler)
enableJIT(3) #maximum optimization of JIT compiler
kellyFast <- cmpfun(kellySensitivity)
kellyFast()
```

R-code 3.3c Sensitivity of Kelly's optimal portfolio to the estimated parameters

In R-code 3.3c we at first assume that μ and σ estimated from the historical DAX data (we have 281 observations of the monthly DAX returns) are genuine. But if it is the case then we can draw a sample of 281 elements from the normal distribution with these μ and σ, estimate the parameters from this sample and they should be close to the genuine parameters. Unfortunately, this is more or less the case only for σ. As to μ, it can readily deviate from the "genuine" value as much as twice and even more. In absolute terms it is still just a little bit. But look at the formula 3.6! If we set, for simplicity, $r = 0$ (which is nowadays nearly the case due to the quantitative easing policy) and get an estimated value of μ that is equal to the half (or double) of the genuine value then the estimated optimal Kelly fraction also halves (or doubles)!
As I ran the R-code 3.3c, I got the optimal Kelly fractions of 92%, 71% and 88% for, respectively, the 1st, the 2nd and the 3rd iteration. So the estimated optimal Kelly fraction shall never be understood too literally. Rather it is our reference point at the beginning of the investment decision. And if in doubt, it is better to overestimate the volatility and underestimate the expected return. In this case we get a lesser Kelly fraction, hence less profit *and less risk*. But if the Kelly fraction is overestimated, we get less profit *but more risk*!

This case study also shows the beauty of the closed form solutions. Though R can do virtually any computational job, an analytic formula can provide us with many useful hints and ideas. Especially we may readily check the solution *robustness*, i.e. its (in)sensitivity to the (small) parameter variations.

Last but not least some new ideas in R-code 3.3c are also worth discussion. First of all we pack the whole business logic in a function by means of $\boxed{\text{kellySensitivity <-function() \{...\}}}$. Once defined, a function can be called everywhere. But in our case the goal is to compile the R-code in order to accelerate it significantly. This is done by the last four commands. We enable all optimization options by $\boxed{\text{enableJIT(3)}}$ then define a complied version of kellySensitivity()-function by $\boxed{\text{kellyFast <- cmpfun(kellySensitivity)}}$ and finally call this compiled version. As you have likely noticed, the compiled code runs much faster.

To finalize this chapter we briefly consider the idea of a *stochastic process*. We will stay in the realm of the *discrete* processes but we also sketch the way to the continuous processes. As usual, we will resort to R and strive for intuitive understanding and practical usage rather than for mathematical rigor.

We have already seen that the normal distribution does not reflect such properties of the DAX returns as heavy tails and volatility clustering, but might be used for the modeling to a first approximation. And if we can model the returns, we can also model the development of DAX. As to returns, they are just a sequence of the independent (and to the first approximation, identically distributed) random variables. Such sequence of the i.i.d. random variables is the simplest discrete stochastic process. As to the DAX value, the settings are not so simple. First of all there is no independence: obviously, the value of the DAX tomorrow strongly correlates with its value today. Also the identical distribution is not the case: even if the returns are i.i.d. the DAX values are not (they are determined by a composition of returns and thus are generally time-dependent). However, it is not really a problem if we have R at hand. We know how to model the returns and how to (re)construct the DAX path from the returns!

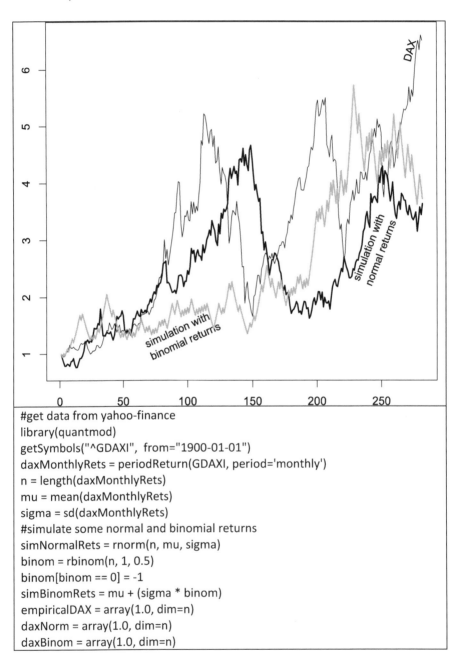

```
#get data from yahoo-finance
library(quantmod)
getSymbols("^GDAXI", from="1900-01-01")
daxMonthlyRets = periodReturn(GDAXI, period='monthly')
n = length(daxMonthlyRets)
mu = mean(daxMonthlyRets)
sigma = sd(daxMonthlyRets)
#simulate some normal and binomial returns
simNormalRets = rnorm(n, mu, sigma)
binom = rbinom(n, 1, 0.5)
binom[binom == 0] = -1
simBinomRets = mu + (sigma * binom)
empiricalDAX = array(1.0, dim=n)
daxNorm = array(1.0, dim=n)
daxBinom = array(1.0, dim=n)
```

```
for( i in 2:n )
{
  daxNorm[i] = daxNorm[i-1] * (1 + simNormalRets[i-1])
  daxBinom[i] = daxBinom[i-1] * (1 + simBinomRets[i-1])
  empiricalDAX[i] = empiricalDAX[i-1] * (1 + daxMonthlyRets[i-1])
}

#plot results
maxY = max(c(daxNorm, daxBinom, empiricalDAX))
minY = min(c(daxNorm, daxBinom, empiricalDAX))
plot(empiricalDAX, type="l", ylim=c(minY, maxY))
lines(daxNorm, lwd=2)
lines(daxBinom, lwd=2, col="grey")
```

Figure 3.9a and R-code 3.4 DAX: historical dynamics for 1990-2014 and two simulated paths with normal and binomial monthly returns

Moreover, due to the Central Limit Theorem it does not matter much whether the returns are normally distributed or not: in the long term the result will be nearly the same. Please note, however, that the CLT may work poorly for the assets that are prone to bubbles and bursts. It should also be applied with caution to the assets whose prices jump and drop too strongly and/or too frequently. But the returns on DAX or Dow Jones are not too volatile. Though they do drop and jump, the severe drops are relatively infrequent (and the high jumps are even more infrequent). Thus it is not implausible to apply the CLT in this case. Let us simulate the DAX dynamics with normally and binomially distributed monthly returns.

In R-Code 3.4 only the lines binom[binom == 0] = -1 and simBinomRets = mu + (sigma * binom) are worth commenting. The former means: "in *binom*-array replace all values that are equal to 0 with -1". The latter generates an array of the simulated returns, which can take two values: either $\mu + \sigma$ or $\mu - \sigma$. As you likely notice at figure 3.9a, the historical and the simulated DAX paths are qualitatively similar. Of course they develop differently (since the returns are stochastic) but there are similar zigzags, similar up and down movements and so on. To put it briefly, if we remove the legend from the figure 3.9 and show it to a person who has never had a look at the DAX chart, he will not be able to distinguish the historical and the simulated DAX paths. Strictly speaking, the simulation path with binomial returns is visually a little bit different since the binomially distributed returns are less irregular than the normally distributed returns (the former can take only two values). But if we shorten the holding period (e.g. switch from the monthly returns to the daily) this difference degenerates, as figure 3.9b shows. I deliberately made no legend and no color difference.

To reproduce[53] figure 3.9b just change two lines in R-code 3.4: replace *period='monthly'* with *period='daily'* in the 4th line and remove *col="grey"* in the last line.

Moreover, even if we stick to the monthly returns (which are more practical for a retail investor who does not trade every day) then it still does not matter much whether we simulate with normal or binomial returns. Indeed, first of all we are interested in [the distributions of] the terminal wealth and the maximum drawdown. R-code 3.5 lets us determine the distribution of these values.
As you readily see at figure 3.10 the densities of the terminal wealth are hardly distinguishable. The terminal wealth is (approximately) lognormally distributed. Since the density of the lognormal distribution is skewed, for a better visibility it makes sense to consider the density of the logarithmic terminal wealth. Indeed, the logarithmic transformation removes the skewness and improves visibility. And as we expected, the densities of the logarithmic terminal wealth are also nearly the same for the normal and the binomial returns. The same holds for the densities of the maximum drawdown (figure 3.11). Note that though the density of the maximum drawdown might look like a normal density, it is indeed not the case.

---

[53] Obviously, the reproduction will never be exact, due to the stochasticity of the simulated returns.

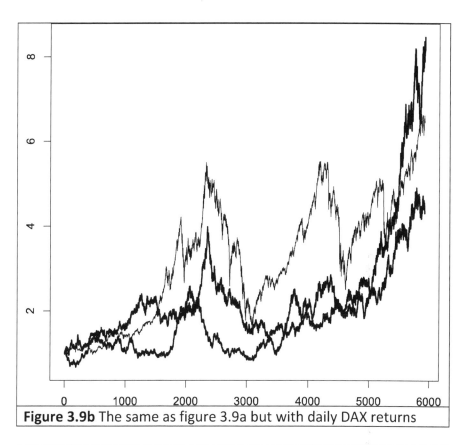

Figure 3.9b The same as figure 3.9a but with daily DAX returns

```
#simulation of the terminal wealth and the maximum drawdown
#run after R-code 3.4a
install.packages("fTrading")
library("fTrading")
N_SIMULATIONS = 1000
terminalWealthNorm = array(0.0, dim=N_SIMULATIONS)
terminalWealthBinom = array(0.0, dim=N_SIMULATIONS)
mddNorm = array(0.0, dim=N_SIMULATIONS)
mddBinom = array(0.0, dim=N_SIMULATIONS)

#simulate many scenarios and record the terminal
#wealth and the maximum drawdown for each
for( k in 1:N_SIMULATIONS )
{
simNormalRets = rnorm(n, mu, sigma)
binom = rbinom(n, 1, 0.5)
binom[binom == 0] = -1
simBinomRets = mu + (sigma * binom)
```

```
daxNorm = array(1.0, dim=n)
daxBinom = array(1.0, dim=n)
for( i in 2:n ) {
  daxNorm[i] = daxNorm[i-1] * (1 + simNormalRets[i-1])
  daxBinom[i] = daxBinom[i-1] * (1 + simBinomRets[i-1])
}
terminalWealthNorm[k] = daxNorm[n]
terminalWealthBinom[k] = daxBinom[n]
mdd = maxDrawDown(daxNorm)
mddNorm[k] = (daxNorm[mdd$to] / daxNorm[mdd$from]) - 1
mdd = maxDrawDown(daxBinom)
mddBinom[k] = (daxBinom[mdd$to] / daxBinom[mdd$from]) - 1
}
#plot the results. Note the better visibility of the terminal log-wealth densities
par(mfrow=c(3,1))
plot(density(terminalWealthNorm), lwd=2)
lines(density(terminalWealthBinom), lwd=2, col="grey")
plot(density(log(terminalWealthNorm)), lwd=2)
lines(density(log(terminalWealthBinom)), lwd=2, col="grey")
plot(density(mddNorm), lwd=2)
lines(density(mddBinom), lwd=2, col="grey")
```

R-code 3.5 DAX: distribution of the terminal (logarithmic) wealth and the maximum drawdown for the normal and binomial returns

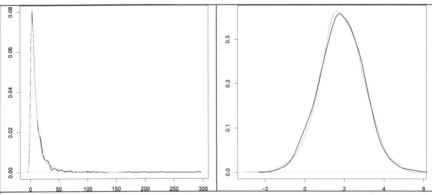

Figure 3.10 Densities of the simulated terminal wealth (left) and the logarithmic terminal wealth(right) : binomial returns (grey) vs. normal returns (black)

In case of the normal returns we can even find an analytical formula for the density of the maximum drawdown. But it is beyond the scope of this book and, as usual, the simulated density is sufficient for the practical purposes.

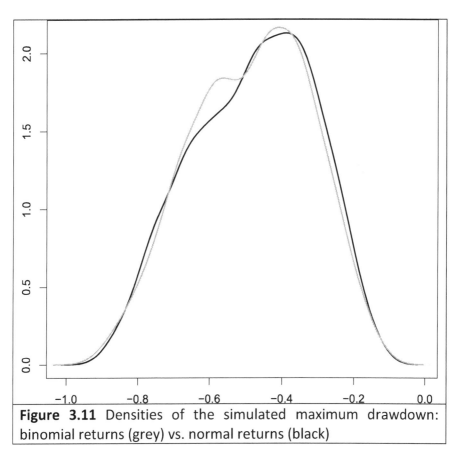

Figure 3.11 Densities of the simulated maximum drawdown: binomial returns (grey) vs. normal returns (black)

Note that a drawdown may be large: a passive investor should prepare himself to a [temporal] loss of more than half of his wealth!

To calculate the drawdown, we used the respective function of the R-library *fTrading*. The function *maxDrawDown* returns a *list*. Lists are similar to arrays; however, their elements are accessed by the keys (or names) rather than by the order numbers. So *mdd* is a list but *daxNorm* is an array, respectively, *mdd$from* and *mdd$to* contain the order numbers of the elements of *daxNorm* with which the period of the maximum drawdown starts and ends.

So far we have seen that the modeling with binomially and normally distributed returns yields similar results. However, we also observed that for the daily returns the similarity was somewhat stronger than for the monthly returns. What happens if we make the holding period shorter and shorter? Let us divide the initial holding period (i.e. a year) to many small sub-periods (months, days, hours, minutes or even ticks) like we did in Q11 of the Quiz. However, the situation is not as simple as in case of the formula 1-A11-1. The return over each (however small) period is stochastic. Thus we may assume the wealth invested in DAX grows according to the <u>*stochastic* differential equation</u> (SDE) $dS_t = S_t(\mu dt + \sigma dW_t)$. Here I abuse my own notation a little bit: in order to conform to the financial mathematics mainstream I write S_t for the wealth process (S_t means stock). As to dW_t it now stands for the "infinitesimal noise" (W_t for the Wiener process, sometimes one also writes B_t for the Brownian motion, which is the same). The theory of the stochastic processes delivers many very interesting and useful results, which may seem counterintuitive at the first glance. In particular, the solution of this SDE is

$$S_t = S_0 \exp([\mu - 0.5\sigma^2]t + \sigma W_t)$$

and not $S_t = S_0 \exp(\mu t + \sigma W_t)$ as you might expect. However, it is actually plausible: recall Q5 from the Quiz: the returns like ±1% are nearly mutually annihilating but we need a return of 100% in order to counterbalance the return of -50%. Thus the term $-0.5\sigma^2$ just tells us that the volatility of returns drives the stock price down!

Last but not least, we have always estimated the market parameters (i.e. the drift μ and the volatility σ) from the historical returns. It is nice in theory but is it really applicable in practice?! Finally, the past and the future are never the same. Well, as to the volatility, you may rely on the past value as a proxy for the future. I have analyzed the historical returns of about 6000 stocks and concluded that in approximately 40% of cases the past volatility does not differ much from the future one (unless a switch from low to high volatility regime occurs but such switches are infrequent and easily recognizable: they take place when Lehman goes bankrupt, Greece discloses its financial problems, etc). 40% of the cases is also not perfect but better than nothing. The next question is what historical period to take for the volatility estimation. It is actually more an art than science. I, for one, usually take the latest year, the latest quarter and the latest month. Quite frequently they do not differ that much. If they do differ significantly and $\sigma_{\text{year}} > \sigma_{\text{quarter}} > \sigma_{\text{month}}$ or vice versa $\sigma_{\text{year}} < \sigma_{\text{quarter}} < \sigma_{\text{month}}$ I consider this tendency and rather take the monthly volatility. In other cases I probably take the $\max\{\sigma_{\text{year}}, \sigma_{\text{quarter}}, \sigma_{\text{month}}\}$ or will not trade the stock at all. Anyway, it does not hurt to add some risk buffer, i.e. (slightly) increase the estimated volatility.

The volatility is crucial not only for the optimal asset allocation according to the Kelly criterion but also for the correct choice of take profit and stop loss orders. The larger is the volatility, the less capital you should invest in this stock and leave the more distance for your orders. Otherwise you will "trade noise", which is (due to the bid-ask spread and the broker fees) an unfavorable game.

As to the drift, the historical values are usually a poor proxy for the future. Moreover, in order to estimate the drift you need the historical data for a long period since in the short term the volatility dominates the drift. Recall e.g. the R-code 3.2d: I got $\mu = 0.0085$ but $\sigma = 0.0605$, i.e. $\sigma >> \mu$ and you should get something like this too. But a long historical period means looking to the long past, which may be obsolete for the present and the future. That's why I usually proceed as follows:

1. I identify the take profit and the stop loss levels (how to do it is another big question that we are going to discuss later)
2. I estimate the probabilities to reach the stop-loss and

take profit. Quite often I just assume the probability of 50% for both events.
3. I calculate the maximal expected growth rate according to the Kelly criterion and consider whether this trade is worthy.
4. Finally, I estimate the maximal holding period (it is not a trivial task which we are also going to discuss later).

Assume that the returns of a stock you are trading are normally distributed with daily drift $\mu = 0.0003$ and daily volatility $\sigma = 0.02$
You are going to buy this stock and hold it for a year.
Determine the optimal Kelly fraction and calculate the probability to experience a drawdown of 5% and 20%.
Do the same calculations with $\mu = 0.006$ and $\sigma = 0.04$

Exercise 3.1 (theoretical trading)

Have a look at the charts of the Metro AG (the largest German retailer). Would you buy this stock right now? If yes, where would you set your stop loss and take profit? Which probabilities would you assign to these events? With chosen stop loss, take profit and their probabilities estimate:
a) the optimal Kelly fraction
b) the probability to reach the SL, TP and none of them
c) the expected length of the holding period

Exercise 3.2 (practical trading)

Do try to solve these exercises by yourself before you look at the sample solutions! Solving by yourself may (and actually will) require a lot of time but this is the only way to get hands-on experience!

Figure 3.12a Metro AG: one year chart and maximum available history chart

Solution to Exercise 3.1

At first we find the optimal Kelly fraction analogous to R-code 3.3a. There is a little difference between R-code 3.3a and R-code 3.6a. First of all we declare *solEx31Part1* as a function with *parameters*. It is very comfortable approach: we need to calculate the optimal Kelly fraction for two different pairs of the drift and volatility, so all we have to do is to call the same function with the different parameters (the last two code lines do it). We also precompile the function to accelerate it, as we did in R-code 3.3c. There are 365 (or 366) calendar days in a year but only about 242 trading days, so we set[54] N_TDAYS = 242.

We get the optimal Kelly fractions of 76% and of 65% for, respectively, the first and the second case.

```
solEx31Part1 <- function(mu, sigma)
{
N_SIMULATIONS = 10000
N_TDAYS = 242 #there are 242 trading days in a year
N_STEPS = 100 #iteratively try 1%, 2%, ... , 100% capital in stock
r = 0.01 / N_TDAYS #daily interest rate

#find optimal Kelly fraction
wealth = array(1.0, dim=c(N_STEPS, N_SIMULATIONS))
meanLogWealth = array(0.0, dim=N_STEPS)
for( u in 1:N_STEPS )
{
  for( i in 2:N_SIMULATIONS)
  {
    monRets = rnorm(N_TDAYS, mu, sigma)
    for(m in 1:N_TDAYS)
    {
      if( monRets[m] < -0.99 ) monRets[m] = -0.99 #truncate
      if( monRets[m] > 0.99 ) monRets[m] = 0.99 #at +/-99%
      portfolioRet = ((u / N_STEPS)*(monRets[m] - r) + (1 + r))
      wealth[u, i] = wealth[u, (i-1)] * portfolioRet
```

---

[54] Strictly speaking, we should have considered all calendar days when dealing with the interest rate r and the drift μ but only the trading days when dealing with volatility σ. Overenthusiastic readers can read a wonderful paper "Why does Stock Market Volatility Change Over Time?" (§V.A "Trading Days and Volatility") by G.W. Schwert available at http://schwert.ssb.rochester.edu/jfin89.pdf

```
   }
  }
  meanLogWealth[u] = mean(log(wealth[u, ]))
 }
 max(meanLogWealth)
 which.max(meanLogWealth)
 }
 #compile before running to speed-up
 require(compiler)
 enableJIT(3) #maximum optimization of JIT compiler
 kellyFast <- cmpfun(solEx31Part1)
 mu1    = 0.0003
 sigma1 = 0.02
 mu2    = 0.0006
 sigma2 = 0.04
 kellyFast(mu1, sigma1)
 kellyFast(mu2, sigma2)
```

R-code 3.6a Solution to Exercise 3.1, part 1

As to the second part, we solve it analogous to R-code 3.3a. Note the values we get: in the first case one gets a drawdown of -20% in more than a half of scenarios and a drawdown of -5% is nearly always the case! And this is for the whole portfolio, i.e. if you invest all capital in stock, the drawdown would be even more severe! In particular, it means that *if you set a stop loss too close to the current stock value, you are going to be knocked-out by the volatility!* Or in other words, *if you do not allow for a sufficiently large [temporal] drawdown, you are trading noise!*

Also note a relatively modest maximal expected growth rate: it is about 3%!   Note that the market parameters are realistic: $242 \cdot \mu = 242 \cdot 0.0003 = 0.0726$ (a not bad expected annual return), $0.02 \cdot \sqrt{242} = 0.31$ (a realistic annual volatility[55]) and $r = 0.01$ is currently a pretty good interest rate for the short term deposits!

As to the second case ($\mu = 0.0006$ and $\sigma = 0.04$) the drawdown and the expected growth rate are even worse, so that the stock is probably not worth trading at all!

---

[55] Recall that for the independent random variables the variance, i.e. σ^2 is additive. When working with volatility, i.e. with σ, we need to scale with a square root.

```
library("fTrading")
solEx31Part2 <- function(mu, sigma, kellyFrac)
{
  N_TDAYS = 242 #number of trading days in a year
  N_SIMULATIONS = 10000
  r = 0.01 / N_TDAYS #daily interest rate

  results = array(1.0, dim=c(N_SIMULATIONS, N_TDAYS))
  drawDown005 = array(0, dim=N_SIMULATIONS)
  drawDown02  = array(0, dim=N_SIMULATIONS)
  for( i in 1:N_SIMULATIONS )
  {
   stockRets = rnorm(N_TDAYS, mu, sigma)
   for( d in 2:N_TDAYS )
   {
    if( stockRets[d] < -0.99 )stockRets[d] = -0.99 #truncate
    if( stockRets[d] > 0.99 ) stockRets[d] = 0.99 #at +/-99%

    portfolioRet = (stockRets[d] - r)*kellyFrac + (1+r)
    results[i, d] = results[i, (d-1)] * portfolioRet
   }
   path = results[i, ]
   mdd = maxDrawDown(path)
   mddValue = (path[mdd$to] / path[mdd$from]) - 1
   if( mddValue  < -0.2)
   {
    drawDown02[i] = 1
    drawDown005[i] = 1
   }
   if( mddValue < -0.05 )
    drawDown005[i] = 1
  }

  #probabilities of -20% and -5% drawdown
  print(sum(drawDown02) / N_SIMULATIONS)
  print(sum(drawDown005) / N_SIMULATIONS)

  #probability density of the term. log-wealth
  terminalLogWealth = log(results[, N_TDAYS])
  print(mean(terminalLogWealth))
  print(sd(terminalLogWealth))
  plot(density(terminalLogWealth))
```

```
}

#compile before running to speed-up
require(compiler)
enableJIT(3) #maximum optimization of JIT compiler
solEx31Part2Fast <- cmpfun(solEx31Part2)
mu1    = 0.0003
sigma1 = 0.02
kellyFrac1 = 0.76
solEx31Part2Fast(mu1, sigma1, kellyFrac1)
mu2    = 0.0006
sigma2 = 0.04
kellyFrac2 = 0.65
solEx31Part2Fast(mu2, sigma2, kellyFrac2)
```

R-code 3.6b Solution to Exercise 3.1, part 2

Solution to Exercise 3.2

Since I regularly watch the stock prices for long periods, I immediately recognize a distinct support level at €27.50. (Whether the support and resistance levels work for trading is another question, I will show you in the next chapter how *you* can verify this. To put it briefly: from my experience the levels are significant, probably just because many traders believe that they are).

There are also two clearly visible levels for take profit: at €30.00 and approximately at €36.00. On the other hand there is no clear level for a stop loss on the one year chart. However, there is such level on maximum-available-history chart: it is €20.00.

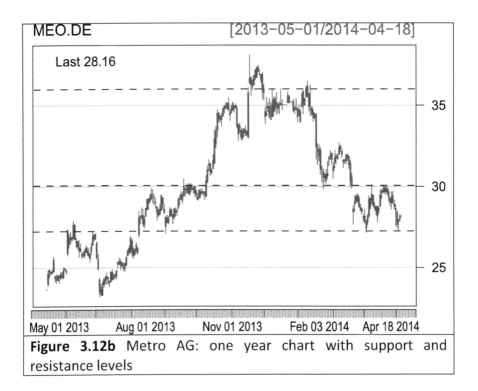

MEO.DE   [2013−05−01/2014−04−18]

Last 28.16

35

30

25

May 01 2013   Aug 01 2013   Nov 01 2013   Feb 03 2014   Apr 18 2014

Figure 3.12b Metro AG: one year chart with support and resistance levels

From figure 3.12b we also conclude that the level of €30.00 could likely be reached within a month or two. As to the level of €36.00, you would probably assume a holding period of about 4 months. However, a jump such as in September 2013 is not a typical phenomenon. For this reason I would suggest considering a holding period of a year...

The choice of probabilities to reach a take profit or a stop loss is even vaguer. Indeed, here we cannot rely exclusively on the stock chart and need some *fundamental* data. As a matter of fact, Metro AG intensively makes business in Eastern Europe and in Russia in particular. Due to the Crimea crisis they postponed the IPO in Russia. Additionally, they made losses in 2013 but on the other hand the forecast for 2014 and 2015 is optimistic and there are reasons to share this optimism: the economy recovers from the crisis 2008 and the low interest rates encourage people to buy consumer goods. However, there are currently a lot of negative

factors as well: Russian-Ukrainian confrontation (that may readily turn into war), Fed is going to start increasing the interest rates gradually (so that a capital will likely flow from stocks to bonds) and the DAX grew more than 20% during the last year without any significant correction. Respectively, the optimism should be modest so I would assume the probability of 60% to reach €36 (+28.5%) and, respectively, 40% to reach €20 (-28.5%). Since the current price of Metro AG is about €28, the reward-risk ratio is 0.6/0.4 = 1.5; however we know that it is the maximal expected growth rate that really counts. In order to find it we need to maximize
$0.6\ln(u(0.285 - 0.01) + 1.01) + 0.4\ln(u(-0.285 - 0.01) + 1.01)$ in u, where ±0.285 = ±8/28 and 0.01 is the risk free interest rate. The maximal expected growth rate is achieved by $u = 0.58$ and is equal to $0.0237 = 2.37\%$, which is actually modest. Moreover, to invest 58% in a *single* stock is too risky. If we invest 10% in the stock, we yield the expected growth rate of 1.42%, for $u = 0.2$ it is 1.77%. It is still better than by deposit but is such a small excess return really worth trading?! Well, if you have a better opportunity then definitely not. But if there is no better opportunity and you manage the portfolio with a long term in mind then it is likely to be worth trading! In the long term 0.77% does mean something, e.g. $(1 + 1.01)^{30} = 1.3478$ but $(1 + 1.0177)^{30} = 1.6927$ i.e. the excess return of 0.77% p.a. will yield $1.6927/1.3478 - 1 = 25.59\%$ more wealth in 30 years. Moreover, do not forget that such an isolated consideration of a single stock is just the initial decision step; the final decision should always be made in portfolio context (s. chapter 5).

There is still another opportunity: buy now and set take profit at €30. The problem is that we do not know where to set the stop loss. But we may proceed from volatility. Now it is time for a short R-script

```
library('quantmod')
getSymbols("MEO.DE")
#stock charts
par(mfrow=c(2,1))
candleChart(MEO.DE, theme='white')
candleChart(MEO.DE, theme='white', subset='last 12 months')

#estimate volatility of daily returns
dailyRets = periodReturn(MEO.DE, period='daily')
n = length(dailyRets)
sigmaALL = round( sd(dailyRets), 4 )
sigmaYear = round( sd(dailyRets[(n-242):n]), 4 )
sigmama6Mon = round( sd(dailyRets[(n-141):n]), 4 )
sigmaQuarter = round( sd(dailyRets[(n-70):n]), 4 )
sigmaMonth = round( sd(dailyRets[(n-23):n]), 4 )
print(paste(sigmaALL, sigmaYear, sigmama6Mon, sep=" "))
print(paste(sigmaQuarter, sigmaMonth, sep=" "))
```

R-code 3.7 Solution to Exercise 3.2: estimation of volatility

I got $\sigma_{all} = 0.0227$, $\sigma_{year} = 0.0187$, $\sigma_{6Mon} = 0.0174$, $\sigma_{quarter} = 0.0169$ and $\sigma_{month} = 0.0140$. So the volatility of this stock does not change much and even if it does, it rather tends to decrease. But as a conservative trader I would assume a daily volatility of 0.02 (recall: it is better to underbet than to overbet). So if we set the stop loss symmetrically to the take profit (i.e. at €26) we will reach it if the drawdown exceeds -2/28 = -7.1%. This is actually a very ordinary drawdown but do not forget that our holding period is just a month. As before, let us assume the probabilities of, respectively, 0.6 and 0.4 to reach the TP and SL by the end of the holding period. Then the expected return is $0.071(0.6 - 0.4) = 0.0142$. Respectively, by 23 trading days in a month we may assume a daily drift of $0.0142/23 = 0.00062$ and you can (re)use the R-codes 3.6a and 3.6b to make all necessary calculations: modify the code[56] setting *N_TDAYS=23*, recompile the

---

[56] Had we made N_TDAYS a parameter (or a global constant outside of the function) we would not need to make this modification. Such considerations are rather relevant for the big software projects and are beyond the scope of this book. However, it will not hurt if you read more on programming and on programming style in particular.

functions by `kellyFast <- cmpfun(solEx31Part1)` and `solEx31Part2Fast <- cmpfun(solEx31Part2)` and finally run `kellyFast(0.00062, 0.02)` (it will return a fraction of about[57] 90%) and then run `solEx31Part2Fast(0.00062, 0.02, 0.9)`
You will yield the expected growth rate of approximately 1%. For a holding period of one month it is not bad; it corresponds to the CAGR of 12.68%. However, you will definitely not invest nearly all your wealth in a single stock, since the black swans[58] do exist and the stock may fall much lower than your stop loss (due to an order slippage or a gap on trade opening). To avoid this black swan risk you may buy a *knock-out certificate*. In this case the stop loss is guaranteed. However, the issuer of the certificate will never take this risk free of charge. Additionally, there is a bid-ask spread thus the implied drift of 0.0062 will actually be less. You may also buy a call option, but this is even more complicated product, since it also depends on implied volatility (i.e. *not* the volatility we calculated but rather the volatility the market anticipates)...

Actually I bought this stock on 04.04.2014 for €29.79 since, firstly, the stock seemed to be going to break the resistance level at €30.00 (it did not) and secondly since the market seemed to ignore the danger of war in Ukraine (it did). I set a take profit at €35.40, a stop loss at €26.40 and both probabilities are set to 0.5
Retrospectively, it may not seem to be a good trade. First of all, the probability of a take profit might be overestimated but even if it is really so high, the expected growth rate of the total capital is still equal to 1.42% (assuming that we invest 10% of the capital in the stock and leave the rest in cash). The nuance is that I have already held another 10% of capital in Südzucker AG, which correlates with Metro AG very modestly. Thus in portfolio context the investment was really not bad. Additionally, I feared to lose the trading

---

[57] To increase the precision you need to increase N_SIMULATIONS until several repeated simulations result in (nearly) the same fraction.

[58] A prominent trader and writer Nassim N. Taleb use this epithet for the "virtually impossible" events (which actually do occur). I highly recommend to read his books.

opportunity: I believed that the stock would break the €30.00 level and such breakouts usually do not occur smoothly but rather take place when a stock jumps. And a purchase at the price level after a jump would likely be unattractive...

By the example of this exercise you have hopefully seen that making a rational trading decision is far from being easy. But there is also another dilemma: to make a non-negligible excess return as a mid- and long term investor you need the low volatility assets (which are pretty hard to find nowadays) or you need to wait for a "nearly perfect" opportunity with very large profit-loss ratio[59]. If you commit short-term trades, you will get opportunities more frequently *and* yield better CAGR due to the compounded interest. The problem is, however, that in this case the trading will soon take all your time. We will further discuss this problem in the chapter on practical trading.

---

[59] Recall, once again, that both drift (or risk-return ratio) and volatility affect the growth rate.

Chapter 4: Backtesting

There are thousands of books and websites that describe the patterns of the technical analysis. There are also enough books and papers that state that the technical analysis does not work (and the markets are efficient). But have you ever asked yourself whether *you* can check these statements?! Finally, it is *your* money at stake. Fortunately, the answer is, in principle, positive and the solution is based on *statistical hypothesis testing*. The main idea of this approach is very well elucidated by the following example. Assume that your child claims he has cleaned his teeth. You formulate a so called *null hypothesis* that your child tells you the truths. Apparently, you can verify it by checking whether your child's toothbrush is wet. If not, you can surely reject the null hypothesis. However, if the toothbrush is wet, it does not prove your null hypothesis; probably your child is a prodigy and knows statistical theory as well, so he just made his toothbrush wet. Respectively, a statistical test can either reject the null hypothesis or show that the results of *this* test do not contradict to the null hypothesis. But "do not contradict" does not necessarily mean "prove".

Let us consider another example, which we have already encountered in the Quiz: assume you want to check whether a coin is symmetric and as you tossed it 10 times you got 10 heads. We know that the number of heads is binomially distributed and the probability to get 10 heads by 10 tosses is equal to 0.1%. In context of a coin toss this probability is considered to be pretty small, so you would likely reject the null hypothesis. This is how a statistical testing essentially works: after a formulation of the null hypothesis one calculates some *test statistic*, which is the realization of a random variable with known distribution[60]. If the probability that the test statistic gets such value is small, the null hypothesis is rejected. This probability is called a *p-value*. Note that the p-value is not the probability of the null hypothesis itself but is the probability

---

[60] In our coin toss example the test statistic is the number of heads. It is binomially distributed.

to obtain the realization of the associated test statistic. There are no formal rules to choose the p-value thresholds but the popular values are 5% and 1%.

For instance, let us test the assumption that the DAX returns are independent. In R-package "lawstat" there is runs-test (aka Wald-Wolfowitz-Test), which we are going to apply.

```
#get data
library(quantmod)
getSymbols("^GDAXI", from=" 1990-11-26", to="2014-04-26")
daxClose = Cl(GDAXI)
daxReturns = ROC(daxClose, type="discrete")
rets = as.numeric(daxReturns)
len = length(rets)
par(mfrow=c(2,2))

#runs-Test (aka Wald-Wolfowitz-Test)
install.packages("lawstat")
library("lawstat")
runs.test(rets[2:len]) #use all available data for the test
acf( rets[2:len], main="whole sample" ) #plot autocorrelation function
runs.test(rets[2:1001]) #test the 1st thousand
acf( rets[2:1000], main="1st 1000" )
runs.test(rets[2000:3000]) #the 3rd thousand
acf( rets[2000:3000], main="3nd 1000" )
runs.test(rets[3000:4000]) #the 4th  (from 2002-11-01 to  2006-10-04)
acf( rets[3000:4000], main="4th 1000" )
```

R-code 4.1 Test for independence of DAX returns

The test result (i.e. the p-value) will obviously depend on the sample that we use as input data. So at first we used all available historical data. Then we applied the runs-test to the 1st, 3rd and 4th thousand of historical returns. Respectively, we got the following p-values: 0.07102, 0.5269, 0.3591 and 0.001744. It means that only in the last case the null hypothesis (i.e. the independence assumption) shall be rejected since the p-value is too small.

However, you should not blindly rely on the test results[61]. Ideally, you should deeply understand how the test works. This, however, would require a deep knowledge of statistical theory and thus impractical for us. But you can also try to look at the data from another "angle of view". In our case you may have a look at the charts of the *autocorrelation functions*.

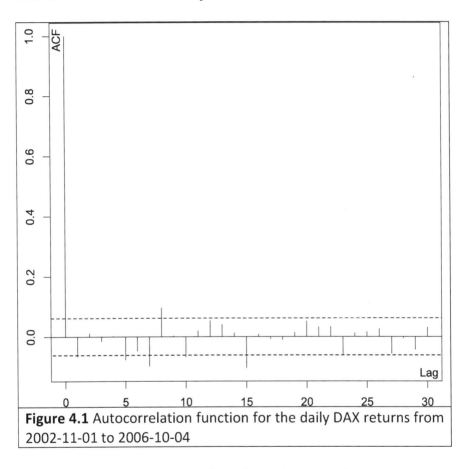

Figure 4.1 Autocorrelation function for the daily DAX returns from 2002-11-01 to 2006-10-04

We consider the idea of the (auto)correlation in detail in the next chapter. So far just note that the correlation is the simplest form of

---

[61] It is ridiculous but many authors of the scientific papers do this mistake. Moreover, it is very common to appeal to a statistical test even when the prerequisites for this test are violated (e.g. many tests imply that the input data are drawn from the normal distribution which often not the case)!

dependence and though it is possible to construct the variables that are dependent but uncorrelated, such constructions are usually artificial. So dependent variables should also be correlated. Figure 4.1 shows that there are some small statistically significant autocorrelations by the lags 7, 8 and 15. It means that the today-return depends on 7-, 8- and 15-days-ago returns. As to other days, the correlations are within the dashed lines, which means that they are statistically insignificant (in a sense, they are due to noise). However, even for the statistically significant lags the correlation is within ±15%, which is really small. Last but not least, we might a-priory expect a correlation with the nearest days (yesterday, probably the day before yesterday) but there is no plausible explanation for an autocorrelation pattern we observed. So I would conclude that in this case a small p-value is likely a statistical artifact rather than a disproof of the null hypothesis.

Probably the most famous application of the statistical hypothesis testing to the technical analysis is the paper "Foundations of Technical Analysis: Computational Algorithms, Statistical Inference, and Empirical Implementation" by Lo, Mamaysky and Wang[62]. They tested whether the distribution of the daily returns, conditioned on ten most popular patterns of technical analysis, are statistically significant. The tested patterns were head-and-shoulders, inverse head-and-shoulders, broadening tops and bottoms, triangle tops and bottoms, rectangle tops and bottoms and double tops and bottoms. The test results were positive, whereas Lo emphasized that "statistically significant" does not yet mean "practically applicable". Moreover, he admitted that if they find something practically worthy they might never publish these results[63]. As you can see, Prof. Lo is a frank person, deservedly being named "a professor with a good head on his shoulders".

---

[62] Published in THE JOURNAL OF FINANCE • VOL. LV, NO. 4 • AUGUST 2000. Available at http://web.mit.edu/alo/www/Papers/1705-1765.pdf
[63] http://www.businessweek.com/stories/2000-04-16/this-alchemy-may-yield-real-gold

Lo, Mamaysky and Wang used advanced statistical techniques and in particular the *kernel regression* (a kind of nonparametric regression). I am not sure that for every reader it is worth trying to reproduce their results. However, if you are curious, you should definitely try; their paper is written very clearly. And of course you do not need to be an expert in kernel regression; the R package *np* will do everything for you.

I, myself, of course tried to reproduce their results ... and came to the conclusion that these technical analysis patterns are *not* significant (or at least, not anymore significant, since Lo tested with the stock prices from 1962 to 1996 and I used more recent data). The R scripts I have written are too long to be put here but they are available from the book's website. After smoothing the historical prices with kernel regression Lo, Mamaysky and Wang formally define the patterns via a sequence of the local maxima and minima. This definition turns out to be flexible but somewhat vague. Indeed, the first example at figure 4.2 is a canonical case of the head-and-shoulders pattern. But the second case hardly qualifies; still it is classified as head-and-shoulders according to Lo's approach. Moreover, they considered only the daily returns after pattern completion but it is a common trading practice to hold a stock (a little bit) longer than just one day. Thus the paper by Lo, Mamaysky and Wang was a bold attempt of scientific approach to the technical analysis but still it leaves a lot of issues open. Though it is principally possible to refine their results, it is not feasible for us since it would require a deep knowledge of the pattern recognition, machine learning and so on. Moreover, the patterns (if used at all) are rather an auxiliary tool of technical analysis. Definitely, the main tool is trends. The support and resistance levels, moving average (crossovers), oscillators like stochastic and MACD and channels like Donchian and Bollinger bands are also frequently used.

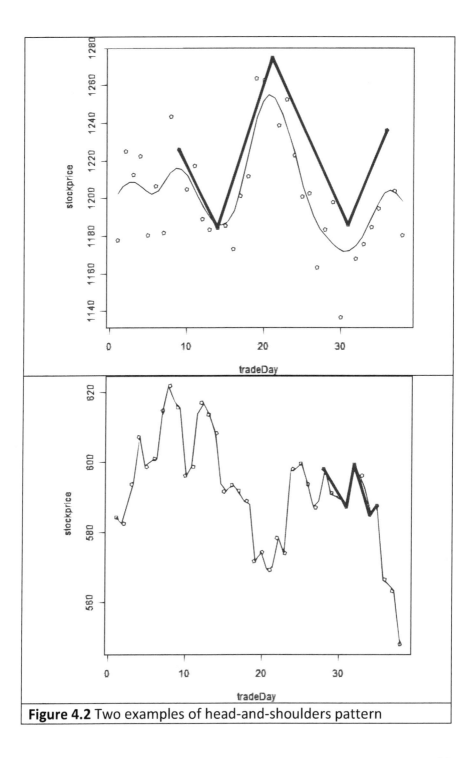

Figure 4.2 Two examples of head-and-shoulders pattern

And these tools can be tested much more easily, especially the oscillators, moving averages and channels, since they are non-ambiguously defined by mathematical formulas. For instance, let us check whether a very frequently recommended approach - buy if the price goes above the 200-days moving average and sell if it drops below - really works.

```
library(quantmod)
#all 30 stocks from DAX
tickers <-c("ADS.DE", "ALV.DE", "BAS.DE", "BAYN.DE",
 "BMW.DE", "BEI.DE", "CBK.DE", "DAI.DE", "DBK.DE",
 "DB1.DE", "LHA.DE", "DPW.DE", "DTE.DE", "EOAN.DE",
 "FME.DE", "FRE.DE", "HEI.DE", "HEN3.DE", "IFX.DE",
 "SDF.DE", "LIN.DE", "MAN.DE", "MRK.DE", "MEO.DE",
 "MUV2.DE", "RWE.DE", "SAP.DE", "SIE.DE", "TKA.DE",
 "VOW3.DE")

#play with different combinations of these parameters!
startDate = '1995-01-01'
endDate = '2014-04-30'
MA_DAYS = 200

getSymbols(tickers, from=startDate, to=endDate)
N_TICKERS = length(tickers)
weatlhDiffs = array(0.0, dim=N_TICKERS)
for( i in 1:N_TICKERS)
{
  closePrices = Cl(eval(parse(text=tickers[i])))
  closePrices = as.numeric(closePrices)
  N_DAYS = length(closePrices)
  MA = SMA( closePrices, MA_DAYS )

  signal = "inCash"
  buyPrice = 0.0
  sellPrice = 0.0
  maWealth = 1.0
  for(d in (MA_DAYS+1):N_DAYS)
  {
    #buy if MA > Stockprice & if not bought yet
    if((MA[d] > closePrices[d]) && (signal == "inCash"))
    {
      buyPrice = closePrices[d]
```

```
      signal = "inStock"
   }

   #sell if (MA < Stockprice OR endDate reached)
   #      & there is something to sell
   if(((MA[d] < closePrices[d]) || (d == N_DAYS))
      && (signal == "inStock"))
   {
      sellPrice = closePrices[d]
      signal = "inCash"
      maWealth = maWealth * (sellPrice / buyPrice)
   }
}
bhWealth = closePrices[N_DAYS] / closePrices[(MA_DAYS+1)]
weatlhDiffs[i] = bhWealth - maWealth
print(paste(tickers[i], weatlhDiffs[i]))

#redirect graphical output to a file
filepath = "D:\\BOOK\\images\\chapter4\\MA200_DAX\\"
filename <- paste(filepath, tickers[i],".png")
png(filename)
ts.plot( closePrices )
lines( MA, col="grey", lwd=2)
dev.off()
}
print(paste("mean wealth Diff: ", mean(weatlhDiffs)))
```

R-code 4.2 Testing whether the SMA200 trading rule really works

At first let us comment the R-code 4.2 and then analyze the backtesting results. The *tickers* is an array, which contains the tickers of all 30 DAX stocks[64]. The command getSymbols(tickers, from=startDate, to=endDate) is already known to us, however, this time we apply it to an array(!) of tickers and specify the start- and end-dates of the backtesting period[65]. The command closePrices = Cl(eval(parse(text=tickers[i]))) is just a

---

[64] A note for a picky reader: the DAX represents *current* 30 largest German companies and is updated from time to time. By the time I wrote this chapter (30.04.2014) the company "MAN" (MAN.DE) was not in DAX anymore.
[65] Unfortunately, for the most of stocks the data on yahoo.finance are available only from 2000 or even later but you will not get any warning message.

technical trick: as a matter of fact after *getSymbols* completes, the price data are stored in the data structures named as the respective tickers: ADS.DE, ALV.DE and so on. But we cannot write just *Cl(tickers[i])* because tickers[i] is considered by R as a string, not as a variable name. That's why we need this *eval(parse(text=tickers[i]))* trick. Further we need to convert *closePrices* from an array of pairs "date, close price" to a numerical array that contains the prices only. We do it by means of closePrices = as.numeric(closePrices) .

In what follows we just implement the MA200 trading rule and compare its performance with buy and hold strategy. In particular, we use a command SMA(closePrices, MA_DAYS) from TTR package[66], which calculates a simple moving average. We also generate the price charts with moving averages like figure 4.3 and write them to a file by means of png(filename) that opens the file for writing and dev.off() that closes it. I got that only for BEI.DE, DBK.DE, DB1.DE, DTE.DE, EOAN.DE, FME.DE, MUV2.DE, SAP.DE the MA200 strategy beats buy and hold. For the other stocks its performance is inferior and on average we would yield 74% less by MA200 than by buy and hold! Actually, we are done with the backtesting and do not need any statistical hypothesis testing since the conclusion is clear: the glorified MA200 strategy fails! Of course you may (and actually should) play with different periods and moving averages. However, you will most likely get the same disappointing results.

---

[66] This packages is automatically installed by the installation of "quantmod".

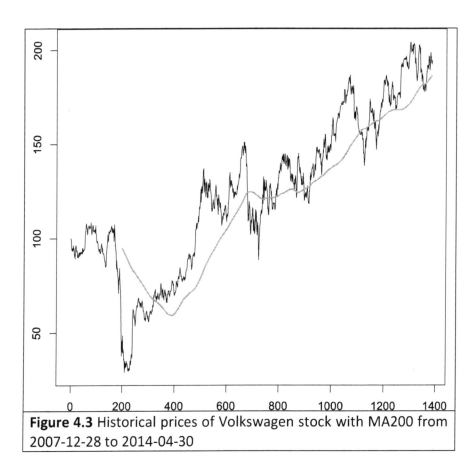

Figure 4.3 Historical prices of Volkswagen stock with MA200 from 2007-12-28 to 2014-04-30

But how about the moving average crossovers?! A moving average crossover works as follows: there are two moving averages, a fast one (usually for 38 days) and a slow one (usually for 200 days). We buy if the fast moving average crosses the slow one from below. Respectively, we sell if the fast moving average crosses the slow one from above. You can readily alter the R-code 4.2 in order to test a MA-crossover strategy. We get that on average the MA-crossover is by 33% better than buy and hold and beats it for the following stocks: ALV.DE, BAYN.DE, CBK.DE, DAI.DE, LHA.DE, DPW.DE, DTE.DE, EOAN.DE, FME.DE, FRE.DE, HEI.DE, HEN3.DE, IFX.DE, LIN.DE, MAN.DE, MEO.DE, MUV2.DE, RWE.DE and SIE.DE

However, it does not prove yet that the MA-crossover strategy is better than buy and hold; finally its superiority might be accidental. To check this we proceed as follows: if the MA-crossover were insignificant the probability to beat buy and hold for each stock would be 50%. We have tested it with 30 stocks and got a superior performance for 19 of them i.e. for 4 stocks more than "on average". The probability that there will be more (or less) than 4 such stocks is calculated by means of $\boxed{1 - (\text{pbinom}(19, 30, 0.5) - \text{pbinom}(11,30,0.5))}$ and is equal to 0.15 which is rather small but still not small enough to reject the null hypothesis that the superior performance of the MA-crossover strategy was accidental. The problem here is that 30 stocks are actually not sufficient for a statistical test. So I just took more stocks and got that the superiority of the MA-crossover *is* significant. However, this result was obtained for the German market and may be invalid for, e.g. the US market. Actually, it is the case, as you can test running R-Code 4.3.

Just like we tested MA200 and MA200+MA38 crossover strategies, you can test oscillators, bands and many other indicators of technical analysis that are implemented in TTR package[67].
Besides all kinds of moving averages and their crossovers I, for one, tested MACD and Stochastic, Donchian Channels and Bollinger Bands, chasing penny stocks and seasonal trading. Simple moving averages, MACD, Stochastic, Donchian Channels and Bollinger Bands simply do not work[68]. MA Crossovers are not bad and pretty robust to the choice of the moving averages but they still cannot beat buy and hold in case of the Dow Jones index.

---

[67] Have a look at http://cran.r-project.org/web/packages/TTR/TTR.pdf
[68] Remember, however, that a trading system usually consists of several indicators that probably do not work standalone but may work together.

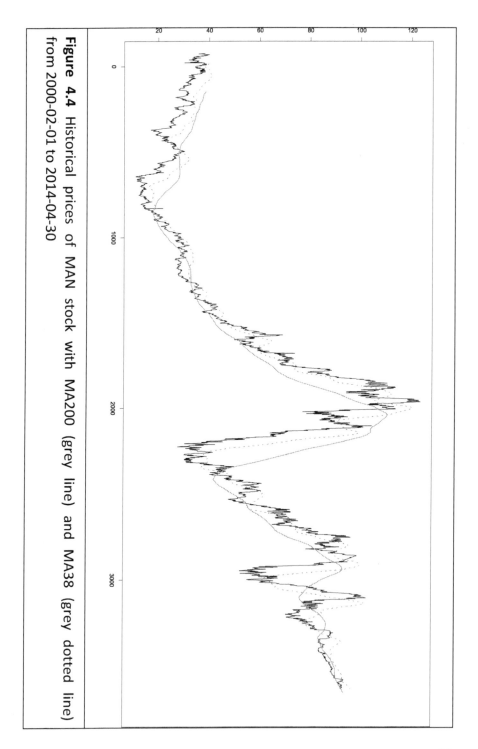

Figure 4.4 Historical prices of MAN stock with MA200 (grey line) and MA38 (grey dotted line) from 2000-02-01 to 2014-04-30

```
library(quantmod)
#all stocks from DowJones IA30 except Merck (6MK.F),
#which caused technical problems
tickers <-c("MMM.F", "ALU.F", "AEC1.F", "SOBA.F",
  "NCB.F", "BCO.F", "CAT1.F", "CHV.F", "CIS.F",
  "CCC3.F", "WDP.F", "DUP.F", "XONA.F", "GEC.F",
  "HWP.F", "HDI.F", "INL.F", "IBM.F", "JNJ.F",
  "CMC.F", "KTF.F", "MDO.F", "MSF.F", "PFE.F",
  "PRG.F", "PA9.F", "UTC1.F", "BAC.F", "WMT.DE")

#play with different combinations of these parameters!
startDate = '1995-01-01'
endDate = '2014-04-30'
MA_DAYS = 200
MA_DAYS_SHORT = 38

getSymbols(tickers, from=startDate, to=endDate)
N_TICKERS = length(tickers)
weatlhDiffs = array(0.0, dim=N_TICKERS)
for( i in 1:N_TICKERS)
{
  closePrices = Cl(eval(parse(text=tickers[i])))
  closePrices = as.numeric(closePrices)
  N_DAYS = length(closePrices)
  MA200 = SMA( closePrices, MA_DAYS )
  MA38 = SMA( closePrices, MA_DAYS_SHORT )

  signal = "inCash"
  buyPrice = 0.0
  sellPrice = 0.0
  maWealth = 1.0
  for(d in (MA_DAYS+1):N_DAYS)
  {
    #buy if MA38 > MA200 & if not bought yet
    if((MA38[d] > MA200[d]) && (signal == "inCash"))
    {
      buyPrice = closePrices[d]
      signal = "inStock"
    }

    #sell if (MA38 < MA200 OR endDate reached)
    #     & there is something to sell
    if(((MA38[d] < MA200[d]) || (d == N_DAYS))
      && (signal == "inStock"))
```

```
   {
     sellPrice = closePrices[d]
     signal = "inCash"
     maWealth = maWealth * (sellPrice / buyPrice)
   }
 }
 bhWealth = closePrices[N_DAYS] / closePrices[(MA_DAYS+1)]
 weatlhDiffs[i] = bhWealth - maWealth
 print(paste(tickers[i], weatlhDiffs[i]))

 #redirect graphical output to a file
 filepath = "D:\\BOOK\\images\\chapter4\\MA_crossover_DJ30\\"
 filename <- paste(filepath, tickers[i],".png")
 png(filename)
 ts.plot( closePrices )
 lines( MA200, col="grey", lwd=2)
 lines( MA38, col="grey", lwd=2, lty=2)
 dev.off()
 }
 print(paste("mean wealth Diff: ", mean(weatlhDiffs)))
```

R-code 4.3 Testing MA200+MA38 crossover for Dow Jones stocks

Chasing penny stocks means losing money for sure.[69] But surprisingly the seasonal trading performed outstanding! The proverb "sell in May and go away" is probably known to everybody but only a few know its second part "but remember to come back in September". This simple rule works very well (it beats buy and hold both for German and US stock markets), however the second part should be specified more precisely: "but remember to come back in *the end of* September".

---

[69] At least if you do it blindly, without doing any fundamental analysis.

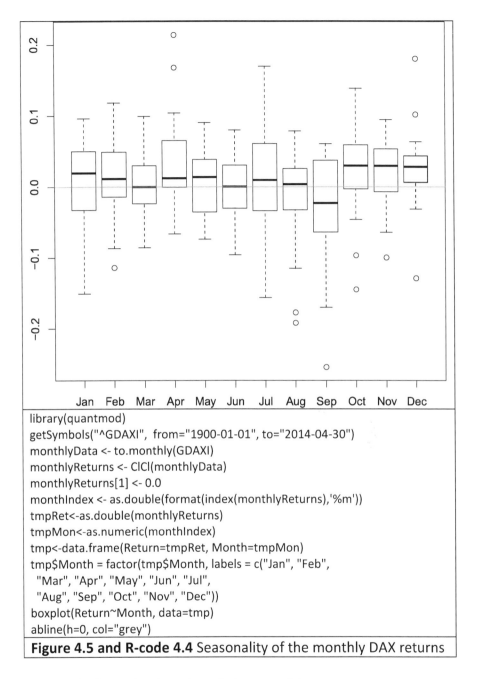

```
library(quantmod)
getSymbols("^GDAXI", from="1900-01-01", to="2014-04-30")
monthlyData <- to.monthly(GDAXI)
monthlyReturns <- ClCl(monthlyData)
monthlyReturns[1] <- 0.0
monthIndex <- as.double(format(index(monthlyReturns),'%m'))
tmpRet<-as.double(monthlyReturns)
tmpMon<-as.numeric(monthIndex)
tmp<-data.frame(Return=tmpRet, Month=tmpMon)
tmp$Month = factor(tmp$Month, labels = c("Jan", "Feb",
  "Mar", "Apr", "May", "Jun", "Jul",
  "Aug", "Sep", "Oct", "Nov", "Dec"))
boxplot(Return~Month, data=tmp)
abline(h=0, col="grey")
```

Figure 4.5 and R-code 4.4 Seasonality of the monthly DAX returns

Have a look at the *boxplot* of the monthly Dow Jones returns. A boxplot displays the median (thick line within the rectangle), the

0.25 and 0.75 quantiles[70] (the lower and the upper bounds of rectangle), whisker (for non-typically large or small values) and sometimes circles (for outliers). The observed seasonality is sometimes explained by a relatively small trading activity in the season of vacations. I would rather argue that the season of vacations generally retards the economy and the stock returns reflect this fact.

Last but not least I would like to discuss two special cases of the backtesting. The first case took place as I saw the following advertisement of a forex trading system in some forum on Linkeln:
- Asset: EUR/USD
- Time frame: mid term
- Trades: 395 (203 long, 192 short)
- Profitable: 64.05%
- Profit : 3725 pips
- Return on initial capital: 37.23%
- Max. drawdown on initial capital: 3.87%

I at first doubted that one can achieve a return of 37.23% by a maximum drawdown of 3.87% and wanted to check it. From the available data we can conclude that the average profit and loss per trade may approximately be ±0.3% since 395 trades * 64.05% profitable = 253 profitable trades, respectively, there are 142 trades with losses and $(1 + 0.003)^{253} \cdot (1 - 0.003)^{142} = 1.3927$

Under this assumption we can model the distribution of the terminal wealth and of the maximum drawdown according to R-code 4.5. As you can see at figure 4.6, the ratio of the drawdown and the profit seems to be plausible. But it certainly does not mean that the advertisement tells us the truth, it merely means that such trading system is, in principle, possible. However, *if* the system performance is true than we have likely guessed the distribution of returns pretty closely. Indeed, the lower is the volatility of returns, the less is possible maximum drawdown. But try to model under assumption that in case of a profitable trade the system makes 1%

[70] Recall that we have already encountered quantiles as we learnt QQplos.

and loses 1.53% otherwise. It still holds that $(1 + 0.01)^{253} \cdot (1 - 0.0153)^{142} = 1.388$ but the expected maximum drawdown will be about 20%!!!

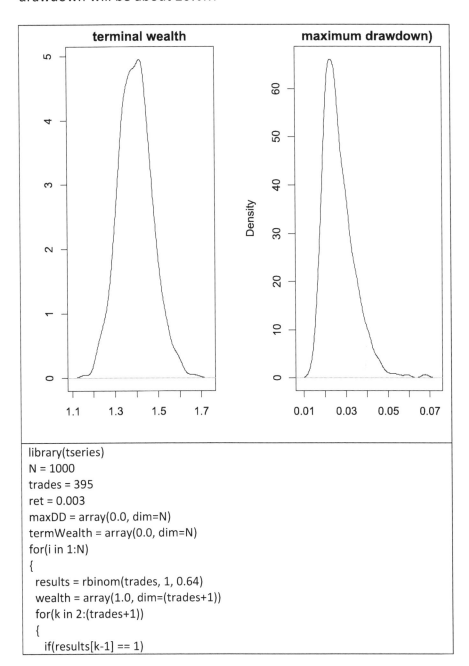

```
library(tseries)
N = 1000
trades = 395
ret = 0.003
maxDD = array(0.0, dim=N)
termWealth = array(0.0, dim=N)
for(i in 1:N)
{
  results = rbinom(trades, 1, 0.64)
  wealth = array(1.0, dim=(trades+1))
  for(k in 2:(trades+1))
  {
    if(results[k-1] == 1)
```

```
      wealth[k] = wealth[k-1] * (1 + ret)
   else
      wealth[k] = wealth[k-1] * (1 - ret )
  }

  maxDD[i] = (maxdrawdown(wealth))[[1]]
  termWealth[i] = wealth[trades+1]
}
par(mfrow=c(1,2))
plot((density(termWealth)))
plot((density(maxDD)))
```

Figure 4.6 and R-code 4.5 Testing the plausibility of a forex trading system

The second case we consider is much simpler. Once I needed to judge the performance of some absolute return fund. It was enough for me to look at figure 4.7 in order to understand that the fund manager is a jerk. Absolute(!) return means a commitment to risk taking, which implies a relatively high volatility. However, it seems that the manager made a kind of adverse asset selection. There is a mixture of the low volatility and the negative returns, i.e. the fund slowly but surely bleeds. Later I read at Morningstar's site that this fund holds a big part of its capital simultaneously in call and put options on EuroStoxx (the index of the 50 largest European companies). It may explain the bleeding: first of all the value of these options decreases with the time and secondly, the stocks (i.e. the underlying) were growing, which usually implies a decrease of implied volatility and thus of the options value!

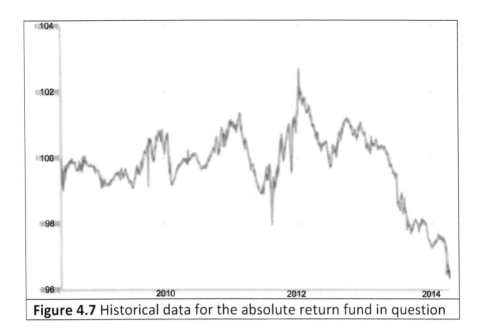

Figure 4.7 Historical data for the absolute return fund in question

The main ideas of the backtesting can be summarized as follows:
1. If the strategy does not work with historical data, it likely will fail by real trading. But even if the historical performance is great, it does not automatically imply that the future performance will be the same (though we may hope for it).
2. Try to test your strategy for as many assets (and asset classes) as possible. It may work for some asset classes and fail for others.
3. If you got disappointing results by backtesting then you are done. But if the results are encouraging, try to formulate a suitable null hypothesis so that you can formally check your results.
4. Do not blindly trust statistical tests. If possible, try several tests and always try to visualize your data and results.

Chapter 5: Multivariate portfolios

So far we have exhaustively studied various trading aspects for a univariate portfolio, i.e. a portfolio that consists of one risky asset (e.g. DAX) and a riskless one (e.g. a bank account or just cash). Actually, such univariate portfolio will likely allow you to achieve 80% of results with 20% of efforts[71]. However, if you want to squeeze everything from the market, you need to structure and diversify your portfolio yourself. The main problem here is the (lack of) time, not the complexity of the underlying theory. All core ideas that we have already discussed for a univariate portfolio remain valid. Additionally, you need to take into account the *correlation* between the assets. In previous chapter we have already encountered the idea of correlation, as we plotted the autocorrelation function for the DAX daily returns at figure 4.1. It showed us that the return today is practically independent of the returns from yesterday, the day before yesterday, etc. But if we consider two or more stocks, their returns will likely be correlated. However, this correlation may be different: the stocks from the same branch usually correlate stronger. Figure 5.1 shows the scatterplots of the daily returns for Deutsche Bank vs. Commerzbank and Deutsche Bank vs. Fresenius[72]. We see that the stocks of both banks are pretty strongly correlated: the scatterplot is strongly elongated, the points are located pretty close to the *regression line*[73] and the *correlation coefficient* is equal to 0.71. As to the case "Deutsche Bank vs. Fresenius", the correlation is much more modest, indeed the correlation coefficient is just 0.25. Note that strictly speaking, the correlation shows only the *linear* dependence and it is possible to give an example of two dependent

---

[71] So-called Pareto principle: http://en.wikipedia.org/wiki/Pareto_principle

[72] Fresenius SE & Co. KGaA is a large pharmaceutical company.

[73] Linear regression fits a straight line between the points so that the sum of squared distances from points to the curve is minimized. If the correlation coefficient is equal to ±1 then all points are located on the regression line.

variables with correlation coefficient equal to zero. However, such constructions are pretty artificial and hardly relevant for us.

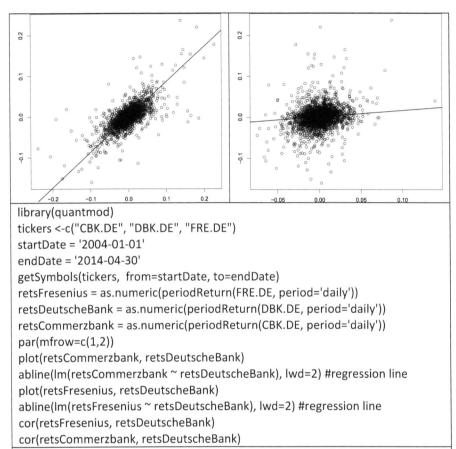

```
library(quantmod)
tickers <-c("CBK.DE", "DBK.DE", "FRE.DE")
startDate = '2004-01-01'
endDate = '2014-04-30'
getSymbols(tickers, from=startDate, to=endDate)
retsFresenius = as.numeric(periodReturn(FRE.DE, period='daily'))
retsDeutscheBank = as.numeric(periodReturn(DBK.DE, period='daily'))
retsCommerzbank = as.numeric(periodReturn(CBK.DE, period='daily'))
par(mfrow=c(1,2))
plot(retsCommerzbank, retsDeutscheBank)
abline(lm(retsCommerzbank ~ retsDeutscheBank), lwd=2) #regression line
plot(retsFresenius, retsDeutscheBank)
abline(lm(retsFresenius ~ retsDeutscheBank), lwd=2) #regression line
cor(retsFresenius, retsDeutscheBank)
cor(retsCommerzbank, retsDeutscheBank)
```

Figure 5.1 and R-code 5.1 Correlation of returns: Deutsche Bank vs. Commerzbank (left) and Deutsche Bank vs. Fresenius (right)

Now let us discuss the idea of correlation more formally. First of all we prove

$$\mathbb{E}[X + Y] = \mathbb{E}[X] + \mathbb{E}[Y]$$

Formula 5.1 The expectation of the sum of random variables

Let X take values in $\{X_1, X_2, \ldots, X_i, \ldots, X_k\}$ and Y in $\{Y_1, Y_2, \ldots, Y_j, \ldots, Y_n\}$ whereas, in general, $k \neq n$. Then there are $k \cdot n$ elementary events such that $\{X = X_i, Y = Y_j\}$. We do not assume that the variables X and Y are independent, so in general
$$p_{ij} := \mathbb{P}(X = X_i, Y = Y_j) \neq \mathbb{P}(X = X_i)\mathbb{P}(Y = Y_j) =: p_i p_j$$

According to the definition 1.1 it holds
$$\mathbb{E}[X + Y] = \sum_{i=1}^{k}\sum_{j=1}^{n}(X_i + Y_j)p_{ij} = \sum_{i=1}^{k}\sum_{j=1}^{n}X_i p_{ij} + \sum_{i=1}^{k}\sum_{j=1}^{n}Y_j p_{ij} =$$
$$\sum_{i=1}^{k}X_i\sum_{j=1}^{n}p_{ij} + \sum_{j=1}^{n}Y_j\sum_{i=1}^{k}p_{ij}$$
But
$$\sum_{j=1}^{n}p_{ij} = \mathbb{P}[X = X_i|Y = Y_1] + \mathbb{P}[X = X_i|Y = Y_2] + \ldots + \mathbb{P}[X = X_i|Y = Y_n] = \mathbb{P}[X = X_i] =: p_i$$
(recall, $\mathbb{P}[X = X_i|Y = Y_1]$ is read "probability that $X = X_i$, given that $Y = Y_1$").

Analogously $\sum_{i=1}^{k}p_{ij} = p_j$ thus
$$\sum_{i=1}^{k}X_i\sum_{j=1}^{n}p_{ij} + \sum_{j=1}^{n}Y_j\sum_{i=1}^{k}p_{ij} = \sum_{i=1}^{k}X_i p_i + \sum_{j=1}^{n}Y_j p_j = \mathbb{E}[X] + \mathbb{E}[Y]$$

Note that we have proved the formula 5.1 both for dependent and independent discrete random variables. Analogously we can prove it for the continuous random variables. Moreover, for any constants a and b it holds

$$\mathbb{E}[aX + bY] = a\mathbb{E}[X] + b\mathbb{E}[Y]$$

Formula 5.1a The linearity of the expectation

But how about the variance? Is there also a nice formula like 5.1a?! Let us check it using the definition 1.2

$$\mathbb{VAR}[X + Y] = \mathbb{E}[(X + Y - \mathbb{E}[X + Y])^2]$$
$$= \mathbb{E}[((X - \mathbb{E}[X]) + (Y - \mathbb{E}[Y]))^2]$$
$$= \mathbb{E}[(X - \mathbb{E}[X])^2 + 2(X - \mathbb{E}[X])(Y - \mathbb{E}[Y]) + (Y - \mathbb{E}[Y])^2]$$
$$= \mathbb{VAR}[X] + \mathbb{VAR}[Y] + 2(X - \mathbb{E}[X])(Y - \mathbb{E}[Y])$$

The value $(X - \mathbb{E}[X])(Y - \mathbb{E}[Y]) =: cov(X, Y)$ is called the *covariance* of X and Y. Note that $cov(X, X) = \mathbb{VAR}[X]$. It can be proved (try to do it using the formula 1-A9-1) that the independent variables have zero covariance. In this case we have a simple formula for the variance of the sum of these random variables.

$$\mathbb{VAR}[aX + bY] = a^2\mathbb{VAR}[X] + b^2\mathbb{VAR}[Y]$$

Formula 5.2 The variance of the sum of independent random variables

However, the independent assets are hardly to find in current globalized markets, thus the formula 5.2 is not very practical for us.

And what if we have more than two correlated random variables?! In this case we have

$$\text{VAR}\left[\sum_{i=1}^{n} a_i X_i\right] = \sum_{i=1}^{n} a_i^2 \text{VAR}[X_i] + 2\sum_{i<j} a_i a_j cov(X_i, X_j)$$

Formula 5.3 Variance of the sum of random variables

Formula 5.3 can also be written in matrix form as

$$(a_1 \quad \cdots \quad a_n) \begin{bmatrix} cov(X_1, X_1) & \cdots & cov(X_1, X_n) \\ \vdots & \ddots & \vdots \\ cov(X_n, X_1) & \cdots & cov(X_n, X_n) \end{bmatrix} \begin{pmatrix} a_1 \\ \vdots \\ a_n \end{pmatrix}$$

where $\begin{bmatrix} cov(X_1, X_1) & \cdots & cov(X_1, X_n) \\ \vdots & \ddots & \vdots \\ cov(X_n, X_1) & \cdots & cov(X_n, X_n) \end{bmatrix}$ is the *covariance matrix.*

Since $cov(X_i, X_j) = cov(X_j, X_i)$ the covariance matrix is *symmetric.* A general shortcoming of covariance as the measure of interdependency is that it depends not only on the interdependence strength as such but also on the individual variances of the random variables. In order to avoid this problem one introduces the *correlation coefficient.*

$$\rho = corr(X, Y) := \frac{cov(X, Y)}{\sqrt{\text{VAR}[X]}\sqrt{\text{VAR}[Y]}}$$

Definition 5.1 Correlation coefficient

It can be proved that $-1 \leq \rho \leq 1$ always holds true. Analogously to the covariance matrix one can specify the *correlation matrix.*

For the probability space in exercise 5.1 calculate:
1. $\text{VAR}[X]$ and $\text{VAR}[Y]$
2. $cov(X, Y)$ and $corr(X, Y)$
3. $\text{VAR}[X + Y]$

Exercise 5.2

Besides the covariance we may also need the second mixed (non-centralized) moment $D(X,Y) := \mathbb{E}[XY]$. In particular, it helps us to find the optimal multivariate portfolio according to the Kelly criterion, it is

$$\vec{u}^{*} = (1+r)(\Sigma)^{-1}(\vec{r} - \vec{1}r)$$

Formula 5.4 Optimal portfolio weights in the sense of Kelly (Nekrasov's formula)

where r is the riskless interest rate, $(\Sigma)^{-1}$ is the inverse of the matrix of the second mixed non-centralized moments of assets excess returns, $\vec{r}$ is the vector of expected asset returns and $\vec{1}$ is the unity vector. The formula 5.4 was invented by me, so I took the liberty of naming it *Nekrasov's formula*[74]. I have also developed a computationally costly but very straightforward numerical algorithm to verify the formula 5.4. Under no leverage and no short selling conditions (i.e. so that all elements of the vector $\vec{u}^{*}$ are between zero and one) we start with a random portfolio. Then we choose another admissible portfolio. If the new portfolio is better, it is set as the new starting point otherwise we return to the previous portfolio. The iteration is repeated until we reach the optimum. For the case of two assets the iteration process is sketched at figure 5.2. Dotted lines mean the unsuccessful choices of the new portfolio, after which we step back.

For a portfolio of two or at most three assets you can also use the brute force portfolio optimization by enumeration. Due to the exponential growth of the computational burden this approach is unfeasible for the larger portfolios. However, it is very straightforward and clear, hence useful too. In particular, it lets us better understand the *beneficial effect of the diversification* (and its limits).

---

[74] The latest version of my working paper "Kelly Criterion for Multivariate Portfolios: A Model-Free Approach" is available at
http://papers.ssrn.com/sol3/papers.cfm?abstract_id=2259133

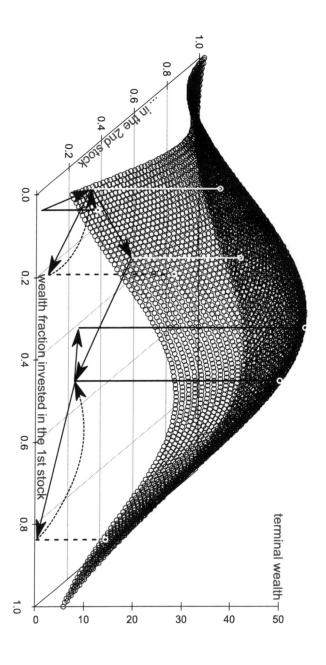

Figure 5.2 Monte-Carlo-Gradient numerical optimization

Let us assume that there are two stocks, both having the expected return of 9% and the volatility of 16%. Additionally, let the risk-free interest rate be 2%, so the excess return of both stocks is equal to 9% - 2% = 7%. The stocks are essentially the same, so may we probably just invest our whole capital in one of them?! Does it really make sense to "disperse" our capital in two stocks and pay more broker fees?! Yes, it does as long as they are not 100% correlated!

We confirm this statement by means of R-Code 5.2. The function estimateSigma allows us to obtain the matrix Σ. Just as the univariate normal distribution is uniquely defined by its expected value μ and standard deviation σ (formula 3.2), the multivariate normal distribution is uniquely defined by the vector of expectations of its components and their covariance matrix. However, there is no analytical way to calculate Σ from the covariance matrix, so we proceed as follows. First we draw a big sample from the multivariate normal distribution with given expectations and covariance matrix by means of the command rmvnorm(n=N, mean=expRets, sigma=covMat) from the package *mvtnorm*. Then we estimate Σ from this sample. Since the sample is large (N = 100000), the estimation of Σ converges to its genuine value. Then we solve the portfolio optimization problem via Nekrasov's formula by means of the command u = (1+riskFreeReturn) * ginv(Sigma) %*% (expRets - riskFreeReturn)
Further we consider all feasible[75] combinations of stock1, stock2 and the risk-free bond and find the best one. Finally we compare the brute force solution with the solution via Nekrasov's formula. They are pretty close to each other[76]: the former tells us to invest 28% in the first stock, 31% in the second stock and the rest in a risk-

---

[75] In the sense of no leverage and no short selling. The elementary step is 0.01, i.e. we consider a portfolio like (0.10, 0.15, 0.75) but not (0.105, 0145, 0.750). For the practical purposes such granulation is more than sufficient.

[76] If you increase the parameter SIMNUM from 100 to 10000 the solutions will become indistinguishable (but the computation will likely last the whole day).

free bond, whereas the latter tells us to put 29% in each stock and the rest in bond. The optimal portfolio yields the cumulated mean growth rate of 3.97 by 100 trades.

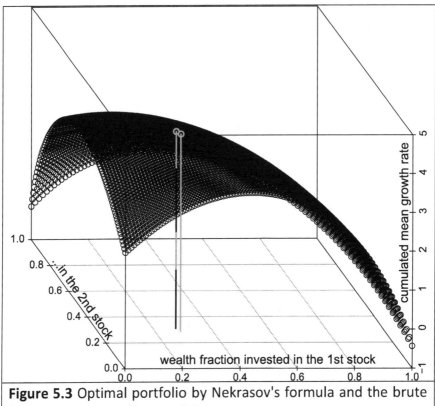

Figure 5.3 Optimal portfolio by Nekrasov's formula and the brute force enumeration for $\rho = 0.5$

Since the stocks are the same in terms of the expected returns and volatilities, the equal portfolio weights of both stocks are plausible. But what happens if we set the correlation coefficient to 1.0?! In this case the optimal solution is to invest just 22% of available capital in each stock. But the maximum cumulated mean growth rate is only 3.46 in this case. Since $\rho = 1.0$ one can also invest 44% of the wealth in any of stock and the expected result will be the same.

For $\rho = 0.0$ we should invest 44% of the capital in each stock and yield the cumulative mean growth rate of 5.3

As you can see, the diversification does help to increase the growth rate but the beneficial effect of the diversification is not unlimited. But additionally, the diversification also reduces the expected maximum drawdown, that's why the indices like DAX or Dow Jones grow much more steadily than the separate stocks that constitute these indices. As a good exercise, you are encouraged to simulate the maximum drawdown of the diversified and undiversified portfolios.

```
#function to estimate the matrix of the second mixed
#non-centralized moments of the excess returns
estimateSigma<-function(inSampleReturns, riskFreeReturn)
{
  n_assets = (dim(inSampleReturns))[1]
  n_observations = (dim(inSampleReturns))[2]
  covMatrix = array(0, dim=c(n_assets,n_assets))
  for(k in 1:n_assets)
  {
    for(j in 1:n_assets)
    {
      covMatrix[k,j] = mean( (inSampleReturns[k,] -
              riskFreeReturn)*(inSampleReturns[j,] - riskFreeReturn) )
    }
  }
  return(covMatrix)
}

#brute force search for the optimal
#portfolio of two risky stocks and
#a riskless bond.
install.packages("scatterplot3d")
install.packages("mvtnorm") #multivariate normal distribution
install.packages("MASS") #matrix inversion
library(scatterplot3d)
library(sm)
library(mvtnorm)
library(MASS)

#parameters:
riskFreeReturn = 0.02
```

```
expRets=c(0.09, 0.09) #expected returns
s1 = 0.16 #standard deviation of returns for the 1st
s2 = 0.16 #...and the 2nd stock
rho = 0.5 #correlation coefficient. Try with rho = 0.0, 0.5 and 1.0 !!!
covMat <- matrix(c(s1, sqrt(s1*s2)*rho, sqrt(s1*s2)*rho, s2),2,2)

# To estimate Sigma we take a BIG sample, so that the estimate
# converges to the genuine value
N = 100000
temp = rmvnorm(n=N, mean=expRets, sigma=covMat)
Sigma<-estimateSigma(t(temp), riskFreeReturn)
#optimal portfolio via Nekrasov's formula
u = (1+riskFreeReturn) * ginv( Sigma ) %*% (expRets - riskFreeReturn)

### detemine the number of all possible fraction
# combinations by no short selling
PATHLEN = 100  #number of trades per path
SIMNUM = 100 #number of repeats (paths)
COMBLEN = 0 #number of admissible fractions
for(i in 0:100) { for(j in 0:(100-i)) { COMBLEN = COMBLEN + 1 } }
terminalWealth = array(0.0, dim=c(COMBLEN, 3, SIMNUM))
##
allFracs<-function()
{
 for( simulation in 1:SIMNUM)
 {
  rets = rmvnorm(n=N, mean=expRets, sigma=covMat)
  for( i in 1:PATHLEN ) #truncate returns at +/-95%
  {
   if( rets[i, 1] < -0.95 ) rets[i, 1] = -0.95
   if( rets[i, 2] < -0.95 ) rets[i, 2] = -0.95
   if( rets[i, 1] > 0.95 ) rets[i, 1] = 0.95
   if( rets[i, 2] > 0.95 ) rets[i, 2] = 0.95
  }
  idx = 1
  for(i in 0:100) {
   for(j in 0:(100-i))
   {
    frac1 = 0.01 * i
    frac2 = 0.01 * j
    wealth = 1.0
    capitalInCash = 1.0 - (frac1 + frac2)
    for( schritt in 1:PATHLEN )
    {
```

```
          wealth =  wealth * ((1.0 + rets[schritt,1])*frac1
          +  (1.0 + rets[schritt,2])*frac2 + 1.02*capitalInCash )
        }
        terminalWealth[idx, 1, simulation] = frac1
        terminalWealth[idx, 2, simulation] = frac2
        terminalWealth[idx, 3, simulation] = wealth
        idx = idx + 1
      }
    }
  }
  return(terminalWealth)
}
library(compiler)
allFracsCompiled<-cmpfun(allFracs)  #compiled R-code runs much faster
terminalWealth=allFracsCompiled()
scatterplot3d(terminalWealth[,,1]) #preliminary scatterplot
#Average among all simulation pathes
terminalWealthAveraged = array(0.0, dim=c(COMBLEN, 3, 1))
for( i in 1:COMBLEN )
{
  terminalWealthAveraged[i, 1, 1] = terminalWealth[i, 1, 1]
  terminalWealthAveraged[i, 2, 1] = terminalWealth[i, 2, 1]
  terminalWealthAveraged[i, 3, 1] = mean(log(terminalWealth[i, 3, ]))
}

#compare theoretical and empirical optimal solutions
s3d<-scatterplot3d(terminalWealthAveraged[,,1], angle=120)
teorMaxIdx = which((terminalWealthAveraged[,1,1]==round(u[1], 2)
  & terminalWealthAveraged[,2,1]==round(u[2], 2))) #from 'of' above
terminalWealthAveraged[teorMaxIdx, ,1]
realMaxIdx = which.max(terminalWealthAveraged[,3,1])
terminalWealthAveraged[realMaxIdx, ,1]
s3d$points(x=terminalWealthAveraged[realMaxIdx,1,1],
   y =terminalWealthAveraged[realMaxIdx,2,1],
   z=terminalWealthAveraged[realMaxIdx,3,1],
   type="h", col="grey", lwd=2, lty=2)
s3d$points(x=terminalWealthAveraged[teorMaxIdx,1,1],
   y=terminalWealthAveraged[teorMaxIdx,2,1],
   z=terminalWealthAveraged[teorMaxIdx,3,1],
   type="h", col="grey", lwd=2)
```

R-code 5.2 Searching for the optimal portfolio of two correlated stocks and one risk-free bond.

Now you [should] clearly understand the main principle of the portfolio diversification and optimal asset allocation. So far, so good. However, the practical application is not as straightforward. First of all we have implicitly assumed that all assets are bought and sold simultaneously. In practice it is, of course, not the case: rather we buy each stock when it becomes especially attractive. Even more important that we do not know the exact value of Σ, we can only approximately estimate it from the market data.

```
#run after R-code 5.2
s1 = 0.4 #volatility of the 1st asset
s2 = 0.3 #..of the 2nd asset
rho = 0.7    #correlation coefficient,  must be in [-1, 1]
mu1 = 0.12   #expected return of the 1st asset
mu2 = 0.09   #..of the 2nd asset
riskFreeReturn = 0.01    #risk-free return
N_SIM = 100 #number of simulations


### theoretical solution with "true" market parameters ###
library("mvtnorm") #multivariate normal distribution
library("MASS")   #[generalized] matrix inverse
covMat <- matrix(c(s1*s1, s1*s2*rho, s1*s2*rho, s2*s2), 2,2)
Sigma<-matrix(c(0.131, 0.067, 0.067, 0.158), 2,2)
expRets = c(mu1, mu2)
print( "Optimal portfolio with TRUE market parameters" )
#optimal portfolio via Nekrasov's formula
u = (1+riskFreeReturn) * ginv( Sigma ) %*% (expRets - riskFreeReturn)
print(u)


##three trias with a limited sample of "emprical" market data##
for( trial in 1:3 )
{
  historicalData = mvrnorm(n=N_SIM, expRets, covMatrix)
  Sigma<-estimateSigma(t(historicalData), riskFreeReturn)
  print( paste("...with EMPIRICAL market parameters - TRIAL ", trial) )
  u = (1+riskFreeReturn) * ginv( Sigma ) %*% (expRets - riskFreeReturn)
  print(u)
}
```

R-code 5.2a Sensitivity of the optimal portfolio to the parameters estimation error

But it turns out that the optimal solution is very sensitive even to the small estimation errors! It would not be a problem if we had a big sample of historical market data. But in practice it is really pretty limited and, moreover, generally we should use the most recent data, since the data from the deep past may be obsolete. To check the sensitivity of the parameter estimation just run the R-code 5.2a. It runs three trials and though the "genuine market parameters" do not change from trial to trial, the results will be different in all three cases (but they will converge if you increase N_SIM).

So does it mean that a pretty complicated theory, which we have considered, is useless in practice?! Definitely not! As far as you recall the chapter 2, it is better to underbet than to overbet. Thus we should always adjust the estimated parameters: increase the (co)variances and decrease the expected returns.

As to non-simultaneous stock purchases and sales, I proceed as follows:
1. I usually trade using support and resistance levels. So I wait until one of the stocks, which I am watching reaches the desired level.
2. From Exercise 3.2 you know how one can estimate the expected return and its variance, as well as the expected holding time. However, it is not sufficient, now we also need to take into account the correlation of our current portfolio and the stock in question. We can estimate this correlation from historical daily data. But we also can rely on common sense: e.g. if we are currently invested in Deutsche Bank then we can buy Fresenius with confidence but we should buy Commerzbank with great caution!

Let us, as usual, consider a concrete example. On 02.05.2014 there were Metro AG (MEO.DE) and Südzucker AG (SZU.DE) in my portfolio. I hold about 10% of my trading capital in each stock. I was watching silver that reached the target level of $19.00 (figure 5.4a). I considered a take profit at $22.00 and a stop loss at $18.40. I have bought Metro AG by €29.79 on 04.04.2014 with take profit at €35.40 and stop loss at €26.40 (recall Figure 3.12b). As to Südzucker AG, I would sell it by €25.00 but there is no predefined stop loss.

First of all I find Südzucker AG attractive for an investment, not just for speculation and secondly I do not see any clear support level. So I am ready to bear virtually any drawdown unless I get a definite reason to sell (this reason may be e.g. a financial statement fraud).

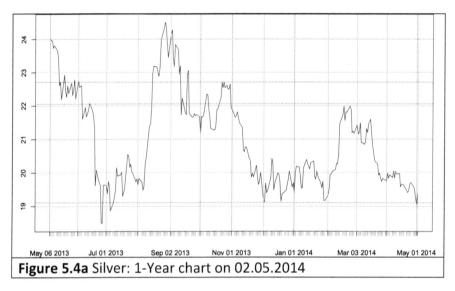

Figure 5.4a Silver: 1-Year chart on 02.05.2014

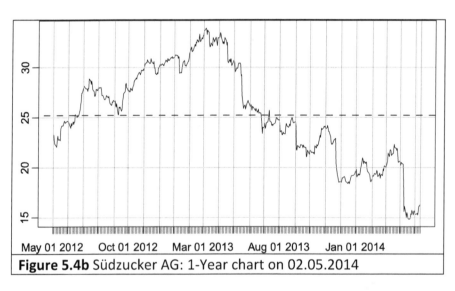

Figure 5.4b Südzucker AG: 1-Year chart on 02.05.2014

So I already have Südzucker AG and Metro AG in my portfolio and need to decide whether (in portfolio context) it is a good idea to buy silver and if yes, how much capital should I invest. As the first step I estimate the correlation matrix of Südzucker, Metro and silver.

```
library(quantmod)
getSymbols(c("MEO.DE", "SZU.DE", "SLV"), from="2013-05-01", to="2014-05-13")
retsMEO = as.numeric(periodReturn(MEO.DE, period='daily'))
retsSZU = as.numeric(periodReturn(SZU.DE, period='daily'))
retsSLV = as.numeric(periodReturn(SLV, period='daily'))
n = min(length(retsMEO), length(retsSZU), length(retsSLV))
retsMatrix = array(0.0, dim=c(n, 3))
retsMatrix[,1] = retsMEO[1:n]
retsMatrix[,2] = retsSZU[1:n]
retsMatrix[,3] = retsSLV[1:n]
corrMat = cor(retsMatrix)
print(round(corrMat,2))
```

R-code 5.3 Estimation of the correlation matrix of Metro AG, Südzucker AG and Silver

Note that the number of available data for the silver and for the stock differs (there are 269 entries for MEO.DE and SZU.DE but only 260 entries for SLV). Probably it is due to different holydays in USA and EU or simply due to some technical problems by Yahoo.Finance. In either case, the difference is not that much significant, however, we need equal number of entries in order to be able to calculate the correlation matrix. So we use this trick with n = min(length(retsMEO), length(retsSZU), length(retsSLV)) Running R-code 5.3 we obtain the following covariance matrix, which I write in a triangle form in order to avoid duplicate values.

	MEO	SZU	SLV
MEO	1.00	0.18	0.06
SZU		1.00	0.01
SLV			1.00

Actually we immediately see that the silver (or, more precisely, *iShares Silver Trust*, a silver ETF) correlates very little both with

Metro AG and Südzucker AG. Since the risk-reward ratio is also good, we are actually done, because the optimal Kelly fraction of silver is definitely more than 10% but I do not invest more than 10% in a single asset[77]! However, for the "pedagogical purpose" we will consider the analysis, which should be done in this case from a formal point of view. So as a starting point we have €1000 in MEO, €1000 in SZU, €8000 in cash and the question is whether SLV is worth buying and if yes then how much we shall invest in SLV. At first we consider SLV separately: we have set the take profit at $22.00, the stop loss at $18.40 and $19.40 is the current price. As you can see at figure 5.4a the support level at $19.00 is very distinct and thus hardly to be broken. Nevertheless, we conservatively assume the probability of 0.5 for both take profit and stop loss[78]. From figure 5.4a we also conclude that SLV may likely reach the take profit level not later than in 6 months. The optimal Kelly fraction[79] would be (more than) 100% but we do not invest more than 10% in one asset; for this capital fraction the expected growth rate is 0.0041 = 0.41% which is not very much.

However, let us look at portfolio context! Since the question is whether or not to buy SLV and, if bought, SLV will be held for 6 months, our planning horizon is 6 months too. First, we simulate the old portfolio. As I bought MEO, I set take profit at €35.40, stop loss at €26.40, the buy price was €29.79 and I assumed the probability of 0.5 for both events. We will simulate the stock dynamics by means of the geometric Brownian motion and need to

---

[77] Strictly speaking, we have disregarded currency risk, since iShare Silver Trust is nominated in USD. But if you have no exposure to specific currency (e.g. a loan that must be repaid in EUR) there is actually no currency risk but rather a currency diversification and in this sense adding SLV to the portfolio is particularly good.
[78] Not only due to a general risk-aversion but also because currently it is still unclear whether a midterm downtrend for silver is broken or not.
[79] Recall figure 2.2 with respective R-code.

find an *implied drift* (i.e. the average daily return, which orresponds to our settings). The easiest way is to find it numerically[80].

```
impliedDrift <-function (buyPrice, TP, SL, TPprob, SLprob, N_DAYS, Vola)
{
 targetUp = TP / buyPrice
 targetDown = SL / buyPrice
 N_STEPS = 100
 N_SIMULATIONS = 100000
 drifts = seq(1, N_STEPS) / 10000 #granulation 0.01%, 0.02% ...
 tpCounts = array(0, N_STEPS)
 slCounts = array(0, N_STEPS)
 resultsArray = array(0, N_STEPS)

 for( d in 1:N_STEPS)
 {
  for( i in 1:N_SIMULATIONS )
  {
   price = 1.0
   rets = rnorm(N_DAYS, drifts[d], Vola)
   for( j in 1:N_DAYS )
   {
    price = price * ( 1+rets[j])

    #break and goto the next iteration
    #if SL or TP is reached
    if( price >= targetUp )
    {
     tpCounts[d] = tpCounts[d] + 1
     break
    }
    else if( price <= targetDown )
    {
     slCounts[d] = slCounts[d] + 1
     break
    }
   }

  }
  tpCounts[d] = tpCounts[d] / N_SIMULATIONS
```

---

[80] Had we worked with logarithmic returns in continuous time, we would be able to find a closed form solution for implied drift.

```
    slCounts[d] = slCounts[d] / N_SIMULATIONS
  }
  resultsArray = abs(tpCounts - TPprob) + abs(slCounts - TPprob)
  optimalDriftId = which.min(resultsArray)
  print( paste( "implied drift: ", drifts[optimalDriftId] ))
  print( paste("empirical TP prob.: ", tpCounts[optimalDriftId] ))
  print( paste("emprirical SL prob.: ", slCounts[optimalDriftId] ))
}

library(compiler)
impliedDriftCompiled<-cmpfun(impliedDrift)
impliedDriftCompiled(29.79, 35.4, 26.4, 0.5, 0.5, 141, 0.01883767)
```

R-code 5.4 Looking the implied drift for MEO

R-code 5.4 does the following: it iteratively takes the daily drift of 0.01%, 0.02%, etc and for each drift we simulate 100000 scenarios. For each scenario we check at every trading day whether we have reached a take profit or a stop loss level. If yes, we increment the counter of respective event and terminate current iteration (we are not interested in stock anymore after the stock price hits a stop loss or take profit). Finally we find the most suitable value of implied daily drift. In our case it is 0.0008 = 0.08%. Its annualized value is $(1 + 0.0007)^{242} - 1 = 21.3\%$, which is much but not implausible. Note that the corresponding probability to reach take profit within six months is equal to 0.49 and the probability to reach stop loss is 0.41. It means that in 100% - 49% - 41% = 10% cases the stock price reaches neither take profit nor stop loss. But 10% is not that much so we may consider the implied drift significant.

As to SZU, we do not have a stop loss level and thus it is harder to choose the implied drift. Still we may consider the historical long term drift, which is 7.5% p.a. i.e. 0.031% per day. It is a pretty pessimistic estimation (I actually believe that there is a potential growth of 20% p.a. and more) but let us stay by it.

Last but not least do not forget that the *current* prices of MEO and SZU are different from the buy prices: both stock prices have decreased by a couple of percents since I bought them. To make the simulation more precise we need to take into account this information. However, there are no big fundamental updates that would make me re-consider my take profit and stop loss levels and/or their probabilities. That's why I run the simulations with old implied drifts but with new prices (i.e. not the buy prices but the current prices are the starting values of the simulated paths).

```
##Old-portfolio##
#run after R-code 5.3
library(mvtnorm)
library(MASS)
library(tseries) #for max. drawdown
volaMEO = sd(retsMEO[1:n]) #is 0.01883767
volaSZU = sd(retsSZU[1:n]) #is 0.02423929
driftMEO = 0.0007
driftSZU = 0.0003
impliedDrifts = c(driftMEO, driftSZU)
rho = cor(retsSZU[1:n], retsMEO[1:n]) #is 0.18
covar = volaMEO * volaSZU * rho
covMatrix = matrix( c(volaMEO^2, covar, covar, volaSZU^2), 2, 2)
N_DAYS = 121 #6 months = half of year = 242/2 trading days
N_SIMULATIONS = 10000
startWealthMEO = 0.1 * 29.35 / 29.79 #10% * current price / buy price
startWealthSZU = 0.1 * 15.70 / 16.10
wealthMEO = array(startWealthMEO, dim=c(N_DAYS, N_SIMULATIONS))
wealthSZU = array(startWealthSZU, dim=c(N_DAYS, N_SIMULATIONS))
wealthCash = array(0.8, dim=c(N_DAYS, N_SIMULATIONS)) #and 80% in Cash
maxDDpath = array(0.0, dim=N_SIMULATIONS) #max. drawdown per path
tpMEO = 0.1 * (35.40 / 29.79)  #€29.79 is the buy price of METRO AG
slMEO = 0.1 * (26.40 / 29.79)
for(i in 1:N_SIMULATIONS)
{
  #pairs of correlated returns
  mRets = mvrnorm(n=N_DAYS, mu=impliedDrifts, Sigma=covMatrix)
  for( d in 2:N_DAYS)
  {
    wealthMEO[d, i] = wealthMEO[(d-1), i] * (1 + mRets[d, 1])
    wealthSZU[d, i] = wealthSZU[(d-1), i] * (1 + mRets[d, 2])
    if( wealthMEO[d, i] >= tpMEO  || wealthMEO[d,i ] < slMEO )
    {
      wealthCash[(d:N_DAYS), i] = wealthCash[(d:N_DAYS), i] + wealthMEO[d, i]
      wealthMEO[(d:N_DAYS), i] = 0.0
    }
  }
}
```

```
    pathWealth = wealthCash[,i] + wealthMEO[,i] + wealthSZU[,i]
    maxDDpath[i] = (maxdrawdown(pathWealth))[[1]]
}
totalWealth = wealthCash + wealthMEO + wealthSZU
terminalWealth = totalWealth[N_DAYS,]
par(mfrow=c(2,1))
print(paste("mean terminal wealth:", mean(terminalWealth)))
print(paste("s.d. terminal wealth:", sd(terminalWealth)))
plot(density(terminalWealth))
print(paste("mean Maximum Drawdown:", mean(maxDDpath)))
print(paste("s.d. Maximum Drawdown:", sd(maxDDpath)))
plot(density(maxDDpath))
```
R-code 5.5a An old portfolio MEO + SZU

The simulation of the new portfolio with SLV is pretty similar. Just
don't forget that now we invest 10% in SLV thus now there is 70% of
capital in cash. In order to find the implied drift by SLV we call
impliedDriftCompiled(19.40, 22.00, 18.40, 0.5, 0.5, 141, 0.01875358) and
obtain an implied daily drift of 0.0015 = 0.15%. This is a little bit too
much but still not implausible, since historically the silver did have
an annual growth of even more than $(1 + 0.0015)^{242} - 1 = 44\%$

```
##New-portfolio##
#run after R-code 5.3
library(mvtnorm)
library(MASS)
library(tseries) #for max. drawdown
driftMEO = 0.0007
driftSZU = 0.0003
driftSLV = 0.0015
impliedDrifts = c(driftMEO, driftSZU, driftSLV)
covMatrix = cov(retsMatrix)# retMatrix comes from  R-code 5.3
N_DAYS = 121 #6 months = half of year = 242/2 trading days
N_SIMULATIONS = 10000
startWealthMEO = 0.1 * 29.35 / 29.79 #10% * current price / buy price
startWealthSZU = 0.1 * 15.70 / 16.10
wealthMEO = array(startWealthMEO, dim=c(N_DAYS, N_SIMULATIONS))
wealthSZU = array(startWealthSZU, dim=c(N_DAYS, N_SIMULATIONS))
#new investment: 10% in SLV
wealthSLV = array(0.1, dim=c(N_DAYS, N_SIMULATIONS))
```

```
wealthCash = array(0.7, dim=c(N_DAYS, N_SIMULATIONS)) #now 70%
maxDDpath = array(0.0, dim=N_SIMULATIONS) #max. drawdown per path
tpMEO = 0.1 * (35.40 / 29.79)  #€29.79 is buy price of METRO AG
slMEO = 0.1 * (26.40 / 29.79)
tpSLV = 0.1 * (22.00 / 19.40)
slSLV = 0.1 * (18.40 / 19.40)
for(i in 1:N_SIMULATIONS)
{
  #pairs of correlated returns
  mRets = mvrnorm(n=N_DAYS, mu=impliedDrifts, Sigma=covMatrix)
  for( d in 2:N_DAYS)
  {
    wealthMEO[d, i] = wealthMEO[(d-1), i] * (1 + mRets[d, 1])
    wealthSZU[d, i] = wealthSZU[(d-1), i] * (1 + mRets[d, 2])
    wealthSLV[d, i] = wealthSLV[(d-1), i] * (1 + mRets[d, 3])
    if( wealthMEO[d, i] >= tpMEO || wealthMEO[d,i] < slMEO )
    {
      wealthCash[(d:N_DAYS), i] = wealthCash[(d:N_DAYS), i] + wealthMEO[d, i]
      wealthMEO[(d:N_DAYS), i] = 0.0
    }
    if( wealthSLV[d, i] >= tpSLV || wealthSLV[d,i ] < slSLV )
    {
      wealthCash[(d:N_DAYS), i] = wealthCash[(d:N_DAYS), i] + wealthSLV[d, i]
      wealthSLV[(d:N_DAYS), i] = 0.0
    }
  }

  pathWealth = wealthCash[,i] + wealthMEO[,i] + wealthSZU[,i] + wealthSLV[,i]
  maxDDpath[i] = (maxdrawdown(pathWealth))[[1]]
}
totalWealth = wealthCash + wealthMEO + wealthSZU + wealthSLV
terminalWealth = totalWealth[N_DAYS,]
par(mfrow=c(2,1))
print(paste("mean terminal wealth:", mean(terminalWealth)))
print(paste("s.d. terminal wealth:", sd(terminalWealth)))
plot(density(terminalWealth))
print(paste("mean Maximum Drawdown:", mean(maxDDpath)))
print(paste("s.d. Maximum Drawdown:", sd(maxDDpath)))
plot(density(maxDDpath))
```

R-code 5.5b A new portfolio MEO + SZU + SLV

Running R-code 5.5a and 5.5b we obtain the following results:

	Old portfolio	New Portfolio
mean terminal wealth	1.0035	1.0086
s. d. of terminal wealth	0.0325	0.0353
mean maximum drawdown	0.0333	0.0336
s. d. of maximum drawdown	0.0123	0.0127

Unfortunately, the numbers are really small thus it is really hard to see the difference. Still you may see that SLV makes the mean terminal wealth slightly better than it makes worse the maximum drawdown. In either case, I wanted to show you a *real* example, so in reality you will mostly confront suchlike numbers!

Your first impression may be that all these trading efforts are merely not worthy. On one hand the expected return of $1.0086 - 1 = 0.86\%$ is really not much. But on the other hand it is for a holding period of 6 months, so the respective annualized return is 1.72% which is twice larger than the current deposit rate.

And it is very important to understand that by our case study we just got started building the portfolio, i.e. sooner or later the [most of] cash will be invested in some *loosely* correlated assets. Let us assume that our portfolio consists of 10 assets and for each asset there are clear take profit and stop loss levels as well as the probabilities to reach them. For the sake of concreteness and simplicity, let us assume that for all ten assets the situation is the same as it was for SLV, i.e. the opportunities are pretty modest.

Additionally, let us assume that all outcomes have a correlation of 20% which is realistic. Let us first model the returns of such portfolio after all 10 assets reach their take profit or stop loss levels.

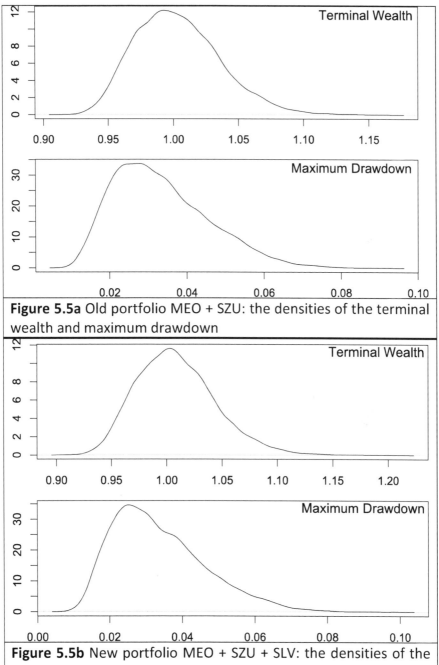

Figure 5.5a Old portfolio MEO + SZU: the densities of the terminal wealth and maximum drawdown

Figure 5.5b New portfolio MEO + SZU + SLV: the densities of the terminal wealth and maximum drawdown

```
install.packages("copula")
library(copula)
N_SIMULATIONS = 100000
CORR = 0.31
RET_UP = (22.00 - 19.40) / 19.40 # = 0.1340
RET_DN = (18.40 - 19.40) / 19.40 # = -0.0515
tmp <- normalCopula( CORR, dim=10 )
x <- rcopula(tmp, N_SIMULATIONS)
b1 = qbinom(x[,1], 1, 0.5)
b2 = qbinom(x[,2], 1, 0.5)
b3 = qbinom(x[,3], 1, 0.5)
b4 = qbinom(x[,4], 1, 0.5)
b5 = qbinom(x[,5], 1, 0.5)
b6 = qbinom(x[,6], 1, 0.5)
b7 = qbinom(x[,7], 1, 0.5)
b8 = qbinom(x[,8], 1, 0.5)
b9 = qbinom(x[,9], 1, 0.5)
b10 = qbinom(x[,10], 1, 0.5)
returns = array(0.0, dim=N_SIMULATIONS)
for( i in 1:N_SIMULATIONS )
{
  if (b1[i] == 0)  b1[i] = RET_DN  else b1[i] = RET_UP
  if (b2[i] == 0)  b2[i] = RET_DN  else b2[i] = RET_UP
  if (b3[i] == 0)  b3[i] = RET_DN  else b3[i] = RET_UP
  if (b4[i] == 0)  b4[i] = RET_DN  else b4[i] = RET_UP
  if (b5[i] == 0)  b5[i] = RET_DN  else b5[i] = RET_UP
  if (b6[i] == 0)  b6[i] = RET_DN  else b6[i] = RET_UP
  if (b7[i] == 0)  b7[i] = RET_DN  else b7[i] = RET_UP
  if (b8[i] == 0)  b8[i] = RET_DN  else b8[i] = RET_UP
  if (b9[i] == 0)  b9[i] = RET_DN  else b9[i] = RET_UP
  if (b10[i] == 0)  b10[i] = RET_DN  else b10[i] = RET_UP

  returns[i] = 0.1 * (b1[i]+b2[i]+b3[i]+b4[i]
       +b5[i]+b6[i]+b7[i]+b8[i]+b9[i]+b10[i])
}
#check that all correlations are about 0.2
mRets <- cbind( b1, b2, b3, b4, b5, b6, b7, b8, b9, b10 )
print(round(cor(mRets), 2))
plot(density(returns))
print(paste("mean return: ", mean(returns)))
print(paste("s.d. of returns: ", sd(returns)))
```

R-code 5.6a Portfolio return after all 10 assets are sold

In R-code 5.6a we use a *Gaussian copula* to generate the correlated binomially distributed random variables. You do not need to know the theory of copulas, for us it is just a technical tool, nothing more. We get the mean return equal to 0.0414 and the standard deviation 0.0491. Let us see which expected growth rate we can achieve with such returns. Running R-code 5.6b we get the expected cumulative growth rate equal to 1.9350, the corresponding terminal wealth is $\exp(1.9350) = 6.92$.

So now the crucial question is *how much time do we need to commit these 10 asset * 50 trades = 500 transactions*?! From figure 5.4a we have assumed that the silver would reach either stop loss or take profit within 6 months. Further, if we trade a *wide* set of assets (stocks, bonds, commodities, currencies), it is not implausible to assume that we can (nearly) always find suchlike opportunities. So one complete portfolio turnover - 10 assets * (1 buy + 1 sell) - takes 6 months. Respectively, 50 trades will take about 25 years. Now recall figure 3.8: for a dollar invested in DAX in 1990, one would yield about 7 dollars after 25 years. This is very close to the terminal value of our portfolio. However, in terms of the maximum drawdown our portfolio is significantly better: we expect the drawdown of -30%, whereas for DAX it once was about -70%!

You may wonder whether it is correct to compare the DAX, which consists of "just" 30 stocks with a portfolio that trades a *wide* set of assets. Certainly, the comparison is not perfect but to some extend it will do: finally, we compare with the *passive* investment in DAX, and a passive investment implies the assets grow over time. This assumption holds for stocks, but unlikely for currencies and commodities, so the diversification opportunities by a passive investment are all the same much more limited. Additionally, the DAX represents the *best* 30 stocks, thus it is very ambitious benchmark.

Last but in no way least let me give you two warnings about correlations. First of all it is not so easy to find uncorrelated assets, nowadays even gold correlates positively with the stock indices! But to find some loosely correlated assets is still realistic. The problem is that they tend to be loosely correlated only *as long as there is no crisis*. And when a crisis comes, the correlations increase abruptly. In other words, almost all assets fall together. This stylized fact is often modeled with *Clayton copula*. Figure 5.7 elucidates the difference: in both cases the marginal returns (i.e. the returns on the 1st and the 2nd asset considered separately) are normally distributed. Moreover, their covariance and correlation matrices are virtually the same. However, in the first case we assume that the assets are *jointly* normally distributed and in the second case we connect them by means of Clayton copula. As you can see, the second case is much more risky: if a crisis comes you cannot count on the diversification effect anymore!

```
#run after R-Code 5.6a
library(tseries) #for max. drawdown
trade = 1
N_TRADES = 50
termWealth = array(1.0, dim=(N_SIMULATIONS / N_TRADES))
maxDD = array(0.0, dim=(N_SIMULATIONS / N_TRADES))

index = 1
while(trade < N_SIMULATIONS )
{
  wealth = array(1.0, dim=N_TRADES)
  rets = returns[trade:(trade+N_TRADES-1)]
  trade = trade + N_TRADES
  for( d in 1:N_TRADES)
  {
    wealth[d+1] = wealth[d] * (1+ rets[d])
  }
  termWealth[index] = wealth[N_TRADES]
  maxDD[index] = (maxdrawdown(wealth))[[1]]
  index = index + 1
}
cgr = log(termWealth)
print(paste("expected cumulative growth rate: ", mean(cgr)))
print(paste("s.d. of cumulative growth rate: ", sd(cgr)))
```

```
par(mfrow=c(2,1))
plot(density(cgr))
plot(density(maxDD))
mean(maxDD)
sd(maxDD)
```

R-code 5.6b Cumulative growth rate of the diversified portfolio after 50 trades

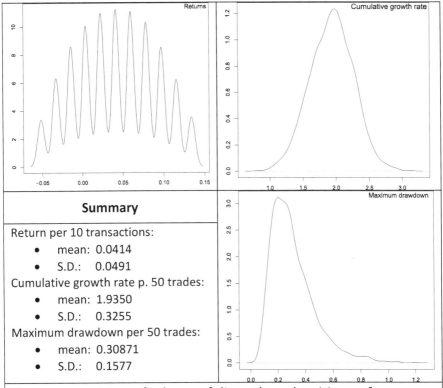

Summary

Return per 10 transactions:
- mean: 0.0414
- S.D.: 0.0491

Cumulative growth rate p. 50 trades:
- mean: 1.9350
- S.D.: 0.3255

Maximum drawdown per 50 trades:
- mean: 0.30871
- S.D.: 0.1577

Figure 5.6 Diversified portfolio: the densities of returns, cumulative growth rate and the maximum drawdown

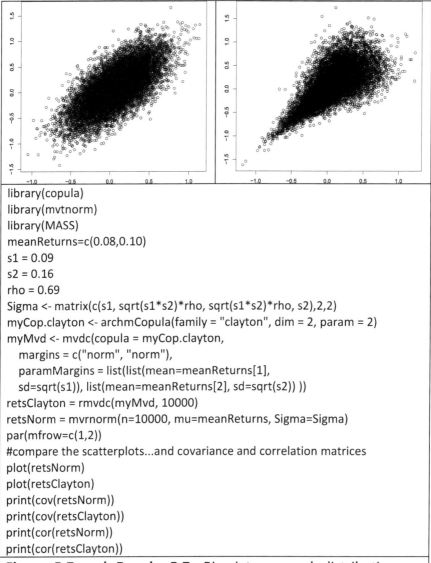

```
library(copula)
library(mvtnorm)
library(MASS)
meanReturns=c(0.08,0.10)
s1 = 0.09
s2 = 0.16
rho = 0.69
Sigma <- matrix(c(s1, sqrt(s1*s2)*rho, sqrt(s1*s2)*rho, s2),2,2)
myCop.clayton <- archmCopula(family = "clayton", dim = 2, param = 2)
myMvd <- mvdc(copula = myCop.clayton,
    margins = c("norm", "norm"),
    paramMargins = list(list(mean=meanReturns[1],
    sd=sqrt(s1)), list(mean=meanReturns[2], sd=sqrt(s2)) ))
retsClayton = rmvdc(myMvd, 10000)
retsNorm = mvrnorm(n=10000, mu=meanReturns, Sigma=Sigma)
par(mfrow=c(1,2))
#compare the scatterplots...and covariance and correlation matrices
plot(retsNorm)
plot(retsClayton)
print(cov(retsNorm))
print(cov(retsClayton))
print(cor(retsNorm))
print(cor(retsClayton))
```

Figure 5.7 and R-code 5.7: Bivariate normal distribution vs. Clayton copula. Danger of the correlation growth in case of crisis.

Chapter 6: Pricing and trading derivatives

Until recently the derivatives were hardly available for the retail investors. Now everyone can buy at least calls and puts as well as knock-outs. Several brokers even allow *selling* [covered] options. Some authors try to make the derivative trading simple but indeed it is a very complicated topic. We will succinctly review the most important valuation and trading issues.

A *call* option is a right (but not an obligation) to buy the underlying (which may be a stock, a bond or even another option) in future (on or up to the expiry date T) for a fixed price K, which is called strike.

An option, which grants a right to buy exactly on T is called *European* option. An option, which allows buying at any time up to T is called *American* option.

Analogously, a *put* option is a right to sell a stock for a given strike K on or up to expiry date T

Definition 6.1 Call and Put options

A *knock-out* is an option, which expires *worthless* if the price of the underlying reaches a certain predefined level (the barrier) within a time span up to the expiry date.

Definition 6.2 Knock-out options

A knock-out option can grant whatever right. But usually the knock-outs for retail investors grant a right at any time t until the expiry to get a payoff equal to $S(t) - K$ (bull knock-outs) or equal to $K - S(t)$ (bear knock-outs), where $S(t)$ is the price of the underlying at time t. Note the similarity of a call option and a bull knock-out as well as of a put option and a bear knock-out!

The options for retail investors[81] are usually issued by the big banks. An option issuer is a *market maker,* i.e. he takes an obligation to quote both buy and sell prices during the trading hours. These prices are often significantly different, i.e. the bid-ask spread is often high.

In order to be a successful option trader you need to understand them and, in particular, be able to judge whether they are cheap or costly. So a natural question is how to price an option. It is a Nobel Prize problem, which was solved by Fischer Black, Myron Scholes and Robert C. Merton. But it were John Cox, Stephen Ross and Mark Rubinstein who made the solution accessible to a general audience by means of their CCR model. Black, Scholes and Merton started with the exponential Wiener Process, which we have very briefly considered in chapter 3. We have also noted that if we model the stock price dynamics with binomially distributed returns over shorter and shorter periods, we converge to the exponential Wiener process. This fact is the starting point of the CRR model. We will learn this model by example.

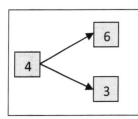

The simplest case: one period CRR model:
- current stock price: €4
- up-outcome: €6, down-outcome: €3
- risk-free interest rate: 5%

Assume that the current stock price is €4 and it can either go up to €6 or down to €3. Further let the risk-free interest rate be 5%. What is the price of the call option with strike €5?!

[81] In Germany they are mostly known as *Optionsscheine* or *Zertifikate*.

The idea is to find a *replicating* (or *hedging*) portfolio, whose payoff is equal to the payoff of the call option in both states. Then the current price of this portfolio should be equal to that of the call option, otherwise there is an *arbitrage opportunity*. Indeed, if currently the option price is larger than the price of the replicating portfolio then we sell the option, hedge the risk *completely* by the replicating portfolio and gain the price difference. Analogously, we buy the option and sell short the replicating portfolio if the option is cheaper.

If the stock goes up, the option's payoff is $6 - 5 = 1$ and if the stock goes down, it is 0 since normally nobody buys a stock for €5 if he can do it for €3. We need to find a portfolio, consisting of α stocks and β bonds and having such payoffs. In order to do this, we just need to solve a simple system of linear equations:

$$6\alpha + 1.05\beta = 1$$
$$3\alpha + 1.05\beta = 0$$

The solution is $(\alpha = \frac{1}{3}, \beta = -\frac{100}{105})$ and the current price of such portfolio is equal to $4 \cdot \frac{1}{3} - \frac{100}{105} \approx 0.38$ which is the *fair price* of the call option. You are likely wondering what $\frac{1}{3}$ of a stock and $-\frac{100}{105}$ of a bond shall mean. Yes, the model assumes that the stocks are divisible, that is one can buy "one third of a stock"[82]. It is also assumed that one can both buy and issue a bond (or deposit and lend money in a bank) at the same interest rate.

Note that the probabilities of up and down movements did not matter at all!

The one period case was really simple, how about a multi period

---

[82] Interestingly, it is not a pure simplification, since the Optionscheine are often issued w.r.t. 0.1 of a stock, i.e. ten Optionsscheine give a right to buy or sell one stock.

model?! Well, it is a little bit more complicated. First of all we need to assign the prices of the underlying asset to all states (tree nodes). Though not necessarily, it is very practical to choose the values in such a way that the up- and down-ratios remain constant. In previous example the up-ratio was $u = \frac{6}{4} = \frac{3}{2}$ and the down-ratio was $d = \frac{3}{4}$. Going on in such a way we become the next states: $S_{uu} = 6 \cdot u = 9$, $\qquad S_{ud} = 6 \cdot d = 4.5$, $\qquad S_{du} = 3 \cdot u = 4.5$ $\qquad$ and $S_{dd} = 3 \cdot d = 2.25$

The advantages of the constant up- and down-ratios are as follows: first of all, you see that it does not matter whether the stock at first went down and then up or vice versa, the terminal price is 4.5 in both cases. In other words, we got a *recombining* binary tree, by which the number of states (or nodes) grows much slowly than by non-recombining trees[83]. And secondly, in case of constant up- and down-ratios we can use the binomial distribution, that is, so to say, reduce the problem to a sequence of coin tosses.

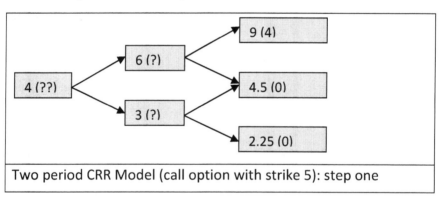

| 4 (??) |
| 6 (?) |
| 3 (?) |
| 9 (4) |
| 4.5 (0) |
| 2.25 (0) |

Two period CRR Model (call option with strike 5): step one

As the next step we proceed with *backward iteration*. It means that at first we determine the option payoff in all terminal states. Then we calculate the value of the replicating portfolio in states S_u and S_d

---

[83] In this example it is not immediately clear but try to sketch a tree with five periods.

For the former we solve:

$$9\alpha + 1.05\beta = 4$$
$$4.5\alpha + 1.05\beta = 0$$

which yields $\alpha = 0.89$ and $\beta = -3.81$ thus in S_u the value of the replicating portfolio is equal to $6 \cdot 0.89 - 3.81 = 1.52$

For the latter we solve:

$$4.5\alpha + 1.05\beta = 0$$
$$2.25\alpha + 1.05\beta = 0$$

and get $\alpha = \beta = 0.0$ which is not surprising since we readily see that once the stock went to S_d, our option *will* expire worthless.

So we have completed the first iteration and now our problem is completely analogous to the one period model:

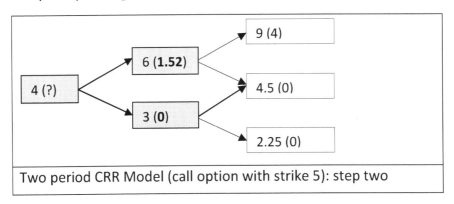

Two period CRR Model (call option with strike 5): step two

$$6\alpha + 1.05\beta = 1.52$$
$$3\alpha + 1.05\beta = 0$$

which gives us $\alpha = 0.51$ and $\beta = -1.45$ thus the option price is equal to $4 \cdot 0.51 - 1.45 = 0.58$

A vigilant reader immediately notices that the option price is larger in case of the two period model. It is actually obvious, since the longer is time to expiry, the more likely the stock price will grow. The second important observation that now it should matter whether we price European or American option. Indeed, compared to the European option, the American option gives us an additional right to buy the stock in state S_u. However, this right brings nothing since we would get $6 - 5 = 1$ but the price of the option in S_u is 1.52

Thus in state S_u it is both rational to hold the option until the expiry or to *sell* it and yield €1.52 (but not to exercise it and get just €1.00). The value which we get by immediate exercise is called *intrinsic value*. The difference between the option price and the intrinsic value is called *time value*.

> It turns out that in case of a call option on the non-dividend(!) paying underlying the value of the American option is equal to the value of the European option, since the early option exercise is irrational.

The non-dividend condition is important! In order to understand it let us extend our model to the third period, in which the stock is going to pay €2 as dividends. Further assume that we landed to the state S_{du} and finally let the strike be equal to €4.00 in this example.

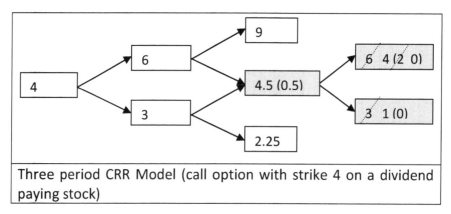

Three period CRR Model (call option with strike 4 on a dividend paying stock)

Since the stock price usually drops (more or less) exactly by the value of paid dividends, our option will be worthless if we hold it to expiry. Thus the early exercise in S_d makes sense, it yields €0.5

At to *put* options, the early exercise possibility does generally matter (whether the stock is paying dividends or not). Consider again the two period model and let the strike be 4. The payoffs in all terminal states are defined as $\max[(4 - S(T)), 0]$

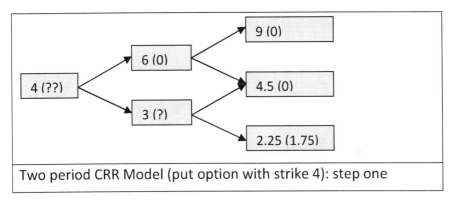

Two period CRR Model (put option with strike 4): step one

Note that the option value in state S_u is obviously zero (since the payoff is zero in this state *and* both in states S_{uu} and S_{ud}).
So let us first find the option value in S_d

$$4.5\alpha + 1.05\beta = 0$$
$$2.25\alpha + 1.05\beta = 1.75$$

The solution is[84] $\alpha = -0.78$ and $\beta = 3.33$. Hence the fair option price in S_d seems to be $3\alpha + \beta = 0.99$. However, if we immediately exercise this option in S_d, we will get a payoff of 1.0! Thus the fair price in S_d is indeed $\max[0.99, 1] = 1$ and if the stock landed to S_d the option should be exercised immediately!

Finally, to calculate the current option price we need to solve

$$6\alpha + 1.05\beta = 0$$
$$3\alpha + 1.05\beta = 1$$

which gives $\alpha = -0.33$, $\beta = 1.90$ thus the current option price is $4\alpha + \beta = 0.58$

---

[84] Note that alpha is negative, i.e. we need to sell the stock short. It is reasonable since buying a put option makes sense when one believes the stock will fall.

Now it is time to make a very important observation! With the up-ratio $u = \frac{3}{2}$, the down-ratio $d = \frac{3}{4}$ and the interest rate $r = 0.05$ we may *define* the following quantity

$$q := \frac{1 + r - d}{u - d} = 0.4$$

Under constraint $0 \leq q \leq 1$ (which is usually the case in practice) we can *let* q be the probability of the up-movement. Then the probability of the down-movement is equal to $1 - q = 0.6$. This is an artificial probability measure, a so-called *martingale* or *risk neutral* measure. It is not inferred from historical stock price data or something like this, it is purely artificial idea (at least at first glance). However, it has a wonderful property: *the price of any option can be expressed as the discounted expectation of its payoff under the martingale measure*!

Let us check this statement for the call option. In S_u the option price is equal to $\frac{1}{1.05}(0.4 \cdot 4 + 0.6 \cdot 0) = 1.52$ and in S_d it is $\frac{1}{1.05}(0.4 \cdot 0 + 0.6 \cdot 0) = 0$. Thus the current fair option price is $\frac{1}{1.05}(0.4 \cdot 1.52 + 0.6 \cdot 0) = 0.58$ i.e. the price via the martingale measure is equivalent to the price via the hedging strategy!

How about puts?! In our example we have in S_u $\frac{1}{1.05}(0.4 \cdot 0 + 0.6 \cdot 0) = 0$ and in S_d we have[85] $\frac{1}{1.05}(0.4 \cdot 0 + 0.6 \cdot 1.75) = 1$, so the value of the option is max[expectation under the martingale measure, payoff by immediate exercise] = max[1,1] = 1. Finally, the current price of the put option is $\frac{1}{1.05}(0.4 \cdot 0 + 0.6 \cdot 1) = 0.57$ (the difference of 0.01 is also due to the rounding error by the calculation of the hedging portfolio).

---

[85] Note that by calculation via the hedging strategy we got 0.99, which is less precise due to the rounding errors by the solution of linear equations. So the solution via the martingale measure is not only faster but is also more precise.

The theory behind the martingale measure is very deep and nontrivial. It is not only a powerful computation tool but it also lets express the *market price of risk*! Black, Scholes and Merton - the luminaries of the option pricing theory - at first knew nothing about the martingale measures. It was Harrison, Krebs and Pliska, who recognized the relation of the hedging strategies (and the no-arbitrage condition) with the martingale measures. Unfortunately we cannot discuss this relation here in detail. But I try to explain informally, how a martingale measure arises. Assume there is a half-blind statistician, who casts a die and wants to determine the probabilities of all events. Indeed the die is symmetric, so all scores from 1 to 6 can appear with equal probability of 1/6. However, our statistician has very poor eyesight and often registers 5 scores when he indeed gets 4 scores, 3 scores when he gets 2 and so on. However, he will never register less than one or more than six scores because he knows that these events are principally impossible. So after he casts a die many times he may get something like the following table:

Scores	1	2	3	4	5	6
Probability	1/6	1/12	1/4	1/12	1/4	1/6

Formally, it is still a valid probability measure, since (1/6 + 1/12 + 1/4 + 1/12 + 1/4 + 1/6) = 1. Somewhat like this the market prices risk: due to the risk preference of the market participants (that are assumed to be equally rational) the real-world probability is distorted so that we get the martingale probability. However, it is very important that the events with zero real-world probability have also zero martingale probability (in this case one can find a transformation of the martingale measure back to the real-world measure[86]).

Now let us apply the martingale measure to the pricing of the knock-outs. Assume that a knock-out payoff is $[S(t) - 3]$ but if

---

[86] The so-called Radon-Nikodym transformation.

$S(t)$ once reaches the value of 3.0 the knock-out immediately expires worthless[87].

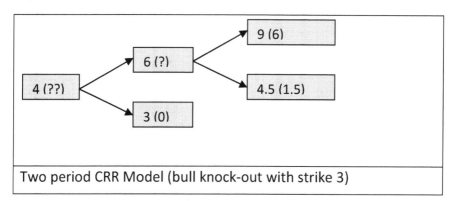

Two period CRR Model (bull knock-out with strike 3)

The questions are what the fair price is and whether to execute the knock-out in S_u or not. In S_u the expected payoff is $\frac{1}{1.05}(0.4 \cdot 6 + 0.6 \cdot 1.5) = 3.14$. An immediate exercise would yield just 3.00 so it is rational to hold the option till the expiry. Respectively, the current fair price is $\frac{1}{1.05}(0.4 \cdot 3.14 + 0.6 \cdot 0) = 1.20$

So we have discussed the fundamental pricing principles of the most common option types that you may encounter as a retail investor. You may wonder whether the CRR model is practical or is it just a toy model for undergraduate textbooks. Yes, it is practical and may be easily calibrated. Let Δt be the model period (a small year fraction) and σ be the annualized stock volatility. Further let r be the annual risk-free interest rate. Set $u = \exp(\sigma\sqrt{\Delta t})$, $d = \exp(-\sigma\sqrt{\Delta t})$ and

$$q = \frac{\exp(r\Delta t) - d}{u - d}$$

and the CRR solution of the call option price will converge to the Nobel Prize Black-Scholes-Merton formula

---

[87] That's why we sketch a truncated tree with the childless node $S_d = 3$

$$C = S_0 \Phi\left(d_1\right) + Ke^{-rT}\Phi\left(d_2\right)$$

$$d_1 := \frac{\ln\frac{S_0}{K} + \left(r + \frac{\sigma^2}{2}\right)T}{\sigma\sqrt{T}}$$

$$d_2 := \frac{\ln\frac{S_0}{K} + \left(r - \frac{\sigma^2}{2}\right)T}{\sigma\sqrt{T}}$$

Formula 6.1 The Black-Scholes-Merton formula

where S_0 is current stock price, K is strike, T is time till expiry, r is interest rate, σ is stock volatility and Φ is the cumulative distribution function of the normal distribution (formula 3.2).

Why is the Black-Scholes-Merton formula so important?! Well, first of all because it is wrong formula in which one puts wrong volatility in order to get a correct option price. Do not laugh, it is a very precise characterization! As the matter of fact all parameters except the volatility are fixed and known at current time. But the volatility is the *implied* volatility for the *future* time span $[\text{now}, \text{now} + T]$. Though the historical volatility is often a good proxy for the implied volatility, they need not to be the same. Moreover, there is a well known phenomenon called *volatility smile*, i.e. on the market there are many options with different strikes and maturities and their prices are known (they are determined by the market). However, there is no single value for the volatility which gives the market prices of all option, i.e. for each option there is the implied volatility $\sigma(K, T)$ that solves the BSM equation in such a way that it gives the current market price of *this* option. In this sense, the BSM Formula lets us *compare* very different options in terms of the implied volatility! A high implied volatility means that the option is expensive. But note that a low implied volatility does not necessarily mean that the option is cheap. Most likely, it is a [call] option on a stock that is going to pay generous dividends.

Secondly, the Black-Scholes-Merton formula allows us to calculate the sensitivities of the option price to the change of stock price, volatility, interest rate and time to expiry. These sensitivities are called Greeks because they are denoted with Greek letters. The most important are: Delta, Gamma, Vega[88], Theta and Rho.

		Calls	Puts
Delta	$\frac{\partial C}{\partial S}$	$\Phi(d_1)$	$\Phi(d_1) - 1$
Gamma	$\frac{\partial^2 C}{\partial^2 S}$	$\frac{\Phi'(d_1)}{S_0 \sigma \sqrt{T}}$	
Vega	$\frac{\partial C}{\partial \sigma}$	$S_0 \Phi'(d_1) \sqrt{T}$	
Theta	$\frac{\partial C}{\partial t}$	$-\frac{S_0 \Phi'(d_1)\sigma}{2\sqrt{T-t}}$ $- rKe^{-r(T-t)}\Phi(d_2)$	$-\frac{S_0 \Phi'(d_1)\sigma}{2\sqrt{T-t}}$ $+ rKe^{-r(T-t)}\Phi(-d_2)$
Rho	$\frac{\partial C}{\partial r}$	$KTe^{-rT}\Phi(d_2)$	$-KTe^{-rT}\Phi(-d_2)$

I borrowed this nice table from Wikipedia[89] just to show you how complicated the formulas are (whereas I must mention that for the financial mathematicians a.k.a. quants these formulas are just a piece of cake). Fortunately you do not need to apply them directly, you may let R and QuantLib do the job for you. QuantLib[90] is a very

---

[88] Which is not a Greek letter.
[89] http://en.wikipedia.org/wiki/Black%E2%80%93Scholes_model#The_Greeks
[90] http://quantlib.org/index.shtml

powerful free/open-source library for the quantitative finance. A part of it is ported to R in package RQuantLib. Though RQuantLib contains only a little bit of QuantLib functionality, it still can do everything you need, i.e. calculate the price and Greeks of the European, American and Barrier options.

However, before we consider an RQuantLib example, let us discuss in simple words what Greeks actually mean. Delta tells us how the option price changes with a (small) change of the price of underlying. For example, if the underlying price changes by -1 and the delta is 0.25 then the option price will change by -0.25. Note that this relation is in absolute terms. In order to get the relative change of the option price in percent, you need to calculate $-0.25/C_0$, where C_0 is the initial option price. Delta also tells you how many stocks you need to buy (or sell) in order to hedge your option, so now the Δ what the α was in CRR model. Recall that the number of stocks may be fractional. Delta of a call option is always between zero and one. Indeed, if the option is deeply *out of the money*, i.e. the strike is much larger than the current stock price, then a small change of the stock price makes virtually no influence on the option price and $\Delta \approx 0$. Oppositely, if an option is deeply *in the money*, i.e. the strike is much smaller than the current stock price then $\Delta \approx 1$.

Gamma tells us how the delta, itself, changes with the change of the stock price (recall that in the CRR model the number of stocks in hedge portfolio changed over time). *At the money options* (with $S(t) = K$) have the largest gamma. Indeed, if $S(t)$ is near K a small change of the stock price may mean a lot and in particular, whether the option expires worthless or will have a positive payoff.

Vega tells us how the option price will change if the [implied] volatility changes. You should never underestimate Vega! It is often the case that the implied volatility decreases when the stock price grows. Thus the price of a call option can go down although the stock price did go up! Vega is positive both for puts and calls, which means that the more volatile is the stock, the more is the expected payoff (we mean the expectation under the martingale measure). However, for the knock-outs it is not the case: indeed, the larger is the volatility, the more is the risk that the knock-out level will be reached. Very edifying example is a so-called European *digital* option, which pays €1 if $S(T) \geq K$ and zero otherwise. As long as $S(t) < K$, Vega is positive (it increases the chance to get $S(\tilde{t}) \geq K$ for $\tilde{t} \in (t,T]$). But as long as $S(t) > K$ the changes of $S(\tilde{t})$ are undesired: a growing stock price does not bring anything and a falling stock price may make the option worthless thus Vega gets negative.

Theta tells you how the option value would bleed if the market stayed motionless. If T is large then Theta is small and vice versa. As well you should never underestimate Theta!

Finally Rho shows the sensitivity to the change of the interest rate. It is less critical than Delta, Vega and Theta, at least in current quasi zero interest rate markets.

You will readily find the RQuantLib documentation in Internet[91]. R-code 6.1 and figure 6.1 provide a small self-explaining example. In this example I also modeled the negative correlation of the stock price and the implied volatility. The most important for me was of course the price. But for the sake of completeness I also plot some Greeks. I am sure that after a thorough consideration of this example you will never underestimate Theta!

I used the R-code 6.1 on 14.02.2014 to model the call optionschein SG32QT on K+S stock. I modeled it with historical volatility. The current theoretical price was even higher than the current market price, as figures 6.1 and 6.2 show[92]. That is, the implied volatility was relatively low, which is a rare case for the deeply out of the money options. Even in spite of a large bid/ask spread the option looked attractive. However, I wanted to model a bad scenario: what

---

[91] e.g. here http://cran.r-project.org/web/packages/RQuantLib/RQuantLib.pdf
[92] Do not forget that this optionschein has the Bezugsverhältnis (exchange ratio, split ratio) 10:1, which means that it is actually an option for 1/10 of a stock.

would have happened if the underlying had just moved ±10% around its current value. After I did my modeling, I definitely decided not to buy this optionschein. Seems to be that I was right!

If you are going to trade options, I do recommend you to play with R-code 6.1 for different option types and parameters!!!

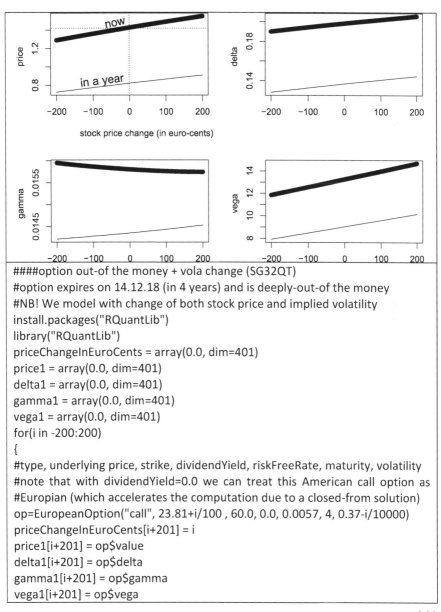

```
####option out-of the money + vola change (SG32QT)
#option expires on 14.12.18 (in 4 years) and is deeply-out-of the money
#NB! We model with change of both stock price and implied volatility
install.packages("RQuantLib")
library("RQuantLib")
priceChangeInEuroCents = array(0.0, dim=401)
price1 = array(0.0, dim=401)
delta1 = array(0.0, dim=401)
gamma1 = array(0.0, dim=401)
vega1 = array(0.0, dim=401)
for(i in -200:200)
{
#type, underlying price, strike, dividendYield, riskFreeRate, maturity, volatility
#note that with dividendYield=0.0 we can treat this American call option as
#Europian (which accelerates the computation due to a closed-from solution)
op=EuropeanOption("call", 23.81+i/100 , 60.0, 0.0, 0.0057, 4, 0.37-i/10000)
priceChangeInEuroCents[i+201] = i
price1[i+201] = op$value
delta1[i+201] = op$delta
gamma1[i+201] = op$gamma
vega1[i+201] = op$vega
```

```
}

#now the same one year later
price2 = array(0.0, dim=401)
delta2 = array(0.0, dim=401)
gamma2 = array(0.0, dim=401)
vega2 = array(0.0, dim=401)
for(i in -200:200)
{
#type, underlying price, strike, dividenYield, riskFreeRate, maturity, volatility
op=EuropeanOption("call", 23.81+i/100 , 60.0, 0.0, 0.0057, 3, 0.37-i/10000)
priceChangeInEuroCents[i+201] = i
price2[i+201] = op$value
delta2[i+201] = op$delta
gamma2[i+201] = op$gamma
vega2[i+201] = op$vega
}

par(mfrow=c(2,2))
tmp = c(price1, price2)
plot(priceChangeInEuroCents, price1, ylim=c( min(tmp), max(tmp) ) )
lines(priceChangeInEuroCents, price2)
tmp = c(delta1, delta2)
plot(priceChangeInEuroCents, delta1, ylim=c( min(tmp), max(tmp) ) )
lines(priceChangeInEuroCents, delta2)
tmp = c(gamma1, gamma2)
plot(priceChangeInEuroCents, gamma1, ylim=c( min(tmp), max(tmp) ) )
lines(priceChangeInEuroCents, gamma2)
tmp = c(vega1, vega2)
plot(priceChangeInEuroCents, vega1, ylim=c( min(tmp), max(tmp) ) )
lines(priceChangeInEuroCents, vega2)
```

Figure 6.1 and R-code 6.1 Modeling the option price and Greeks

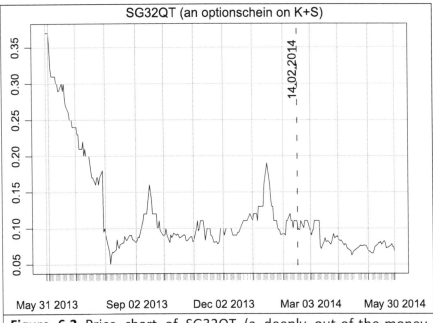

Figure 6.2 Price chart of SG32QT (a deeply out-of-the-money option on K+S)

Chapter 7: Psychology, time management, technical equipment and other aspects of practical trading

If you carefully read the previous chapters then, congratulations, you possess all necessary theory for the portfolio management. But unfortunately this theory is though necessary but far not sufficient and we come to the most important part, the practical one. As you likely anticipate, you may encounter the following problems:

1. Psychological stress
2. Addiction to trading (probably)
3. Lack of time
4. Poor quality of historical data
5. Undercapitalization and considerable broker fees

Let us start with good news: unless you are going to trade intraday, you will hardly confront the fourth problem. Once I compared the daily OHLC data from Yahoo Finance and from Bloomberg[93] almost for all stocks from DAX, mDAX, sDAX and TecDAX. With few exceptions the data were authentic. Of course you should always critically check the data from Yahoo Finance against other sources (e.g. ariva.de) but once again, the data quality will infrequently be an issue.

As to the lack of time, you will likely confront it only if you are going to trade not just indices but rather try to choose the best individual stocks. If you just trade DAX (and, additionally, a couple of commodities like oil and gold or currencies like EUR/USD/JPY) an hour per day to read and watch the news should be enough.

As to the psychological stress, it may (and likely *will*) be a real problem! First of all the discipline and the statistical analysis are

---

[93] Bloomberg and Reuters are two main providers of the financial data for the institutional investors.

boring but gambling is exciting (at least for the most of us). The lack of patience is a very common problem, especially if you are a newbie, you may be too eager to start trading when you should rather wait for a better opportunity. Even worse in this sense is that almost every unleveraged trade needs some time (from several weeks to a couple of years) to be completed. Ideally, you should make a trade, set take profit and stop loss orders and do not look at this trading position anymore unless there are some really(!) important news that may make you reconsider your orders. But most of investors do not behave ideally, instead they watch, watch and watch their positions, being distracted from family, job and so on. The situation will be particularly bad in case of a highly risk-averse person, and it was my case seven years ago! As I made my Master in Germany, my financial abilities were very limited. They were sufficient for two years that I needed to complete my studies but I had to count every cent. Of course I did not trade as I was a student since I did not want to risk the indispensable. But as I graduated from the university, I quickly found a good job so the money was not an acute problem for me anymore. However, due to the inertness of mind I continued to count every cent. On the other hand I understood clearly that the financial crisis, which occurred soon after I found a job, is a good opportunity to make money by trading. I also understood that the trading experience can be very helpful for my career (by that time I was a quantitative software developer but wanted to change to a trading desk or to the risk management). I also wanted to apply my knowledge of derivatives in practice. I was really eager to trade but have coped with my impatience and waited for a good opportunity. And I got it; it was a call optionschein on Adidas (figure 7.1). I patiently waited until some stock(s) correct(s) after a vehement growth in April 2009. My patience was rewarded, the correction of Adidas was pretty strong. I also knew that the implied volatility grows when the stock falls, so I did not try to buy the option exactly when the price of underlying reached the bottom, it would be hardly possible all the same.

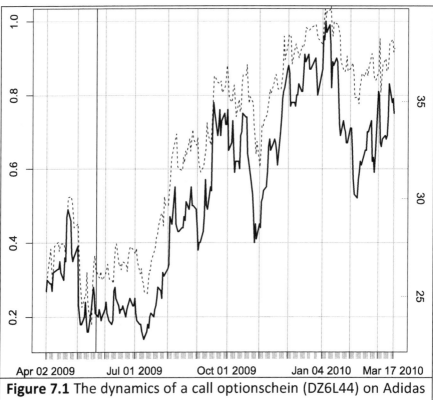

Figure 7.1 The dynamics of a call optionschein (DZ6L44) on Adidas and Adidas itself (dashed line)

Instead, I waited until the implied volatility calmed down and then bought the optionschein on 15.05.2009. Had I just patiently waited until expiry, I would yield about 300% on this trade! But the problem was my extreme risk aversion! Though the sum I invested was really ridiculous - just €100 - it made a lot of pain to me. I could not concentrate on anything; the risk to lose this shitty €100 has obsessed me completely, though I could afford losing of even €1000 without any serious aftermath. So I just waited until I could sell my optionschein with a minimal profit (I did wish to complete my first trade with profit). The gross profit was about €15. What remained after the subtraction of €12 broker fees was sufficient only for a bottle of a cheap sparkling wine, which I drank with my colleagues to my first "profitable" trade.

Later I have thoroughly reflected upon this trade. I continued trading and did learn to consider the invested money as potentially lost money. I estimated that a loss of (up to) €5000 would have no aftermath for me and I traded so conservatively that my position never exceeded this threshold. In other words, even in the highly unrealistic case of a *total* loss I would not breach my limit.

Many behavioral finance researchers argue that it is typical for a human being to pick up the small profits but tolerate the huge drawdowns with a (vain) hope that they will soon recover. For me it never was a problem to cut losses, probably because I was aware of the table from the Quiz/Q5. My readiness to cut losses did save me some thousands of €uro. But it was very hard for me to stop taking profits prematurely! Very gradually and by means of the bitter experience I learnt to let profits grow. Probably the most painful case was my trade in NVIDIA stock (figure 7.2). With this trade I made about 10% profit though I could have made much more!

But as I learnt trading it took more and more time of mine. I made profit, which was not really hard in extremely bullish market in year 2010. But my girlfriend complained that I was thinking only about my trades. During my office hours I also needed all my will to get rid of trading ideas and concentrate on job. Then I got a child and children cost both time and money! I mean that first of all I was not able to concentrate on my trades, just forget it when a baby cries (and you have no idea why). Secondly, my girlfriend had to look after baby and I was a sole wage earner. Moreover, we needed to move to a new apartment and to buy a lot of costly baby accessories. In this context I again became extremely risk-averse. I still tried to continue trading but as soon as I saw that my returns deteriorated I stopped. I am very happy that I did not experience any addiction to trade, probably because I was completely busy with my kid and with my new job. *But do not underestimate the danger of addiction and think twice before your get started with trading*!

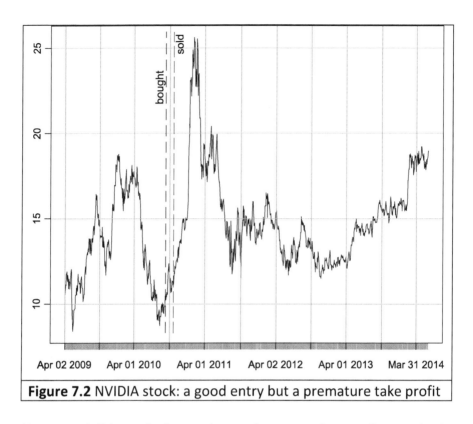

Figure 7.2 NVIDIA stock: a good entry but a premature take profit

However, I did watch the market and once made a perfect trade. In 2011 nobody really believed that S&P would downgrade the US sovereign rating from AAA to AA+. Neither did I, though I considered such scenario as highly improbable but not impossible.

Short before the "judgment day" I observed that the VIX was reaching a strong support at 15.00. Of course it could break this level and fall further but the VIX is a *volatility* index and some volatility is always there. Especially this decrease was highly implausible for the turbulent markets. So opened one long CFD position[94] at 15.20 (nearly a perfect entry) and after the 5th of August 2011 I got it! Unfortunately, I could afford only one CFD position, as I already said, being father and sole wage earner made me somewhat short of money.

---

[94] One cannot buy the VIX itself but it is possible to buy a future on it. Some brokers also offer the CFDs (contracts for difference).

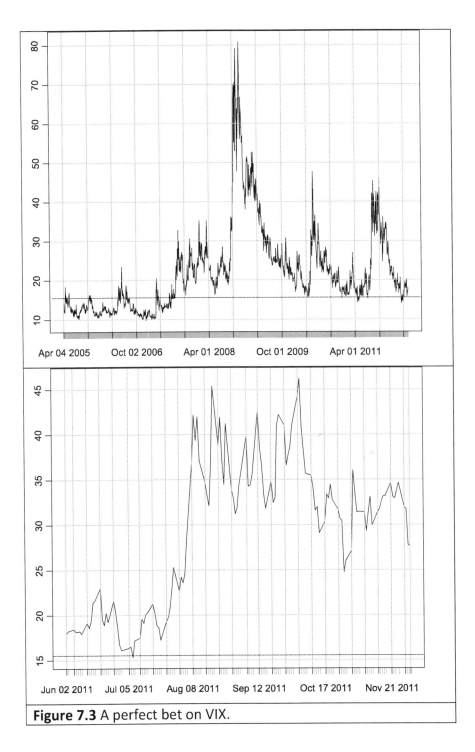

Figure 7.3 A perfect bet on VIX.

I thought that even if S&P did not downgrade the US rating, the VIX would hardly fall further since it was already too low. But still I could not completely disregard this scenario due to my high risk aversion.

Alas, I lost the most of my profit with the next trade: as markets crashed after 05.08.2011 I thought they will quickly recover. Finally, the downgrade was just a more or less subjective decision of the S&P agency and it was not a nuclear meltdown in Fukushima[95] or the bankruptcy of Lehman Brothers. So I got long in DAX but the market continued to fall and triggered my stop loss. After reflecting upon this trade I come to the conclusion that my euphoria was to blame. After a long break I just forgot that *after a good trade one should at first calm down*. Also considering the decision of the S&P as "purely subjective" was a little bit naive, since it automatically made the portfolios of many financial institutions more risky from the regulators point of view. Thus these institutions had to sell a part of risky assets like stocks in order to reduce the market risk exposure.

But in either case these trades have inspired me to get back to trading. My daughter got a little bit older and thus calmer, but we still were short of money and could not invest much. So in order to increase my motivation I decided to write a Ph.D. thesis on trading from the retail investor's view. The goal was twofold, first of all I wanted to systematize my mosaic theoretical and practical knowledge of trading. Secondly, I hoped a Ph.D. will help my career[96]. The most important result of my research is definitely that I have learnt and extended the Kelly criterion. Before I did it, I was able to trade successfully but it was more like a voodoo craft. Intuitively I understood the risk of overbetting but I did not know

---

[95] After which, by the way, the markets recovered very quickly.

[96] It did, but indirectly. I definitely overestimated the German obsequiousness to Ph.D. (in German "Doktortitel") but working on a Ph.D. thesis spoke for my passion for financial markets, which was appreciated. Additionally, I learnt R in detail, which turned out to be very useful as well.

where the overbetting really begins. Now both you and I do know it and this is crucial for a success in the long term!

Enough of my story! Let us get back to you, my dear reader! If you are an advanced student new to the financial markets but eager to learn them, I can also recommend my way to you. If you learn markets, you *will experience* a thrust to trade. As a disciplined person, you may try to suppress it. But there is a risk that your motivation and passion for investment will be suppressed as well. But alternatively you can define your monthly pocket money budget and gamble with it. Just never bet the whole money at once. I would also recommend making at most two bets per month. Additionally, do not gamble with calls and puts unless you understand them. For a beginner I would recommend the knock-out certificates, they are easier to trade. By such approach learning the market will be a fun for you and it is likely that your pocket money will start increasing soon. At the same time you should make a *paper trading* in stocks with the long term in mind. It may take several years before you start making systematic profit with your paper trading. Several years is a lot of time, but the employers will definitely appreciate your efforts as you graduate. I know the dozens of MSc. and Ph.D. graduates in (quantitative) finance who know very advanced mathematical models but never traded a stock and, moreover, do not even know where the DAX currently is! Surely their chances on employment are not particularly good. My recommendation to get the first experience in trading is relevant not only for the students in finance but also for the mathematicians and physicists. You, esp. the physicists, are beloved in financial institutions but contrary to the finance students your potential employers do not expect a deep knowledge in finance. However, *if* you demonstrate such knowledge, you will exceed their expectations! And psychologically they tend to hire a Ph.D. in physics with some basic trading skills than an MSc. in finance with (from their point of view) insufficient practical experience, although measured "on absolute basis" a finance graduate surely knows much more relevant stuff than a physicist...

On the other hand if you are not a student but a "hobby" investor, who already has some knowledge of trading and bought this book to extend it you may probably decide that the trading is not worth your efforts. This is in no way a coward or loser attitude! Conversely, I expect that the most of rational readers (*that are not going to make a career in finance*) will make this decision! Finally, you have seen that the trading is far from being trivial and requires a lot of efforts.

However, a complete avoidance of the financial markets is also suboptimal, at least by the current time of zero risk free interest rates and non-zero inflation. A good idea for a conservative investor is to invest in a well-diversified ETF with low management fees. Rabbi Issac bar Aha have proposed around the fourth century, that one should "put a third in land (real estate), a third in merchandise (stocks) and a third in cash (bonds)". This advice is still sound enough, more than 1600 years later! Some even argue that nowadays it still remains unbeatable[97].

I would, however, state that nowadays the Rabbi's approach is probably the easiest that still works but not the best. As a matter of fact, the developed and emerging markets are different, small caps and big caps are different as well. Thus the idea to put 1/3 in stocks is indeed ambiguous. There are also commodity and currency markets. The problem is, however, that an individual investor needs to make a lot of efforts in order to understand these markets and recognize their trends. Whether to invest in an actively managed fund or in a passive ETF is in no way a trivial decision as well. Some actively managed funds do outperform the market and the most known one is probably the Berkshire Hathaway Inc. However, the past performance is no guarantee for the future. Moreover, essentially Berkshire = Buffet and Buffet is already 83 years old. On the other hand, a passive fund generally replicates the development

---

[97] http://finance.yahoo.com/news/naive-diversification-vs-optimization-163550886.html

of the markets. A broadly diversified passive fund usually performs well in the long run, since in long-term the markets grow with the world economy. And a self-evident advantage of such fund is a small management fee[98]. However, a good diversification is crucial, e.g. investing just in a stock index may be not enough (have a look at the chart of Japanese Nikkei 225).

But if you decided to actively manage your wealth, let me give you some final advices:

1. Start gradually with indices. If in doubt, do not trade, wait for the right opportunity! Although rare they do come! I have already told you about my perfect trade with a CFD on VIX. Currently I am working in energy industry and recently there was another suchlike opportunity: I was pretty sure that the civil war in Ukraine would break out but the gas price on German market was particularly low, so to go long in natural gas was particularly attractive. And indeed, as soon as the Crimea has reunited with Russia, the gas prices jumped. Notably, only for a short time but it would be enough to make a good profit.

2. A perfect opportunity may come very sudden, even if you trade only indices that are relatively low volatile. However, there are such events like the Flash Crash on 06.05.2010 (which I, myself, experienced live). Another good example is the Volkswagen stock: a short squeeze in October 2008 drove it from €200 to over €1000 but just for a few hours. That's why you should buy an LTE-Tablet, install the trading app and be always ready to commit a trade!

3. If you see that the trading with indices brings you profit and fun rather than losses and stress, you may try to pick up the

---

[98] A good passive investment fund can offer small fees because there are no expensive "performance fees". There are still some transaction costs: in order to keep the fund well-diversified, the assets should be re-allocated from time to time. However, the re-allocation is usually infrequent (either by the end of the year or in special cases like Lehman Brother's bankruptcy or the downgrade of US sovereign credit rating).

best stocks, or more general, the best assets (recall Rabbi Issac bar Aha as well as figure 5.6). But beware, your time expenditures may explode at this stage! Also remember that single stocks are much more volatile than indices. If you trade with single stocks, do read the annual reports. I do not want to give you any tips how to do it (maybe I will do it in a sequel to this book ☺). But so far just read them carefully and try to read between lines. For example, if an energy company claims to use derivatives only for hedging, complains low electricity prices but the derivative exposure is negative then be careful: the derivatives were engaged for speculation, not for hedging. Or if a bank reports a good outlook but makes a lot of business in countries like Italy and Spain then you probably should be cautious. But even if you read straightforwardly, you will learn a lot. Finally, the companies are obliged by the regulators to disclose their main risks and the possibilities of the window dressing (in German "Bilanzverschönerung") are limited.

4. When you trade currencies, you do not trade currencies as such but you trade the CFDs (contracts for difference) on them. The same holds for commodities unless you trade directly the ETCs or futures. Essentially, CFDs just multiply your profits and losses with a leverage factor. In particular, it means that you can lose more than your initial deposit! The problem is that some brokers cheat. Indeed a CFD broker should hedge your position on the market (of course not your individual position but rather the net position of all customers). But some brokers (actually they are so-called *bucket shops*) do not hedge, de facto they play against their customers, hoping that a customer will overbet (with leverage it is *very* easy) and lose. Such brokers simply deliver you the non-genuine quotes. In particular, if you set a stop loss, they may trigger it. Of course with the CFDs on indices like DAX the cheating possibilities are limited, since a customer has a clear reference and may complain to a regulator (in Germany it is BaFin: Bundesanstalt für

Finanzaufsicht). But for the currencies there are no such references so a broker can cheat a lot. But even if your broker does hedge, he usually charges the so-called rollover costs (in German "Finanzierungskosten"). Indeed, in order to hedge your leveraged long position a broker needs to borrow money. Although current interest rates like EURIBOR and EONIA are close to zero, a broker usually takes a surcharge of about 3%, which is not negligible. Note that if you hold a leveraged *short* position, a broker shall *pay* you an interest (because in order to hedge he also sells short with leverage and can deposit money). But usually a broker "pays" something like EURIBOR - 3% and since this number is currently negative, the broker effectively either pays nothing or even charges you! The good news is that some brokers do not charge the rollover costs for some products. But this can be done only for the CFDs on futures! In order to hedge with futures a broker just needs a safety margin, which is much less than the position size. Obviously, the brokers (and thus you) need to re-margin if the market makes a relatively big move against you.

5. Be careful with broker fees! By trading derivatives and CFDs be aware of the bid/ask spread and rollover costs! The main advantage of the leveraged instruments like knock-outs and CFDs is that they allow you to make use of relatively small market movements and thus to trade more often. But by a frequent trading the spreads, rollover costs and broker fees will not be negligible! Of course I do not affirm that they make leverage useless, I just encourage you to take them into account when you simulate your trades by means of the Monte Carlo method, like we did in chapters 3, 4 and 5.

I wish you a good luck!!!

Manufactured by Amazon.ca
Bolton, ON

27589491R10087